Let's Hear It for the Boys

What boys really think about school and how to help them succeed

Gary Wilson

BLOOMSBURY EDUCATION
LONDON OXFORD NEW YORK NEW DELHI SYDNEY

BLOOMSBURY EDUCATION
Bloomsbury Publishing Plc
50 Bedford Square, London, WC1B 3DP, UK

BLOOMSBURY, BLOOMSBURY EDUCATION and the Diana logo are trademarks of
Bloomsbury Publishing Plc

First published in Great Britain, 2021

Text copyright © Gary Wilson, 2021

Gary Wilson has asserted his right under the Copyright, Designs and Patents Act, 1988,
to be identified as Author of this work

Bloomsbury Publishing Plc does not have any control over, or responsibility for, any
third-party websites referred to or in this book. All internet addresses given in this book were
correct at the time of going to press. The author and publisher regret any inconvenience
caused if addresses have changed or sites have ceased to exist, but can accept no
responsibility for any such changes

All rights reserved. No part of this publication may be reproduced or
transmitted in any form or by any means, electronic or mechanical,
including photocopying, recording, or any information storage or retrieval
system, without prior permission in writing from the publishers

A catalogue record for this book is available from the British Library

ISBN: PB: 978-1-4729-7463-1; ePDF: 978-1-4729-7460-0; ePub: 978-1-4729-7462-4

2 4 6 8 10 9 7 5 3 1 (paperback)

Typeset by Newgen KnowledgeWorks Pvt. Ltd., Chennai, India
Printed and bound in the UK by CPI Group Ltd, Croydon CR0 4YY

All papers used by Bloomsbury Publishing Plc are natural, recyclable products from wood
grown in well managed forests and other sources. The manufacturing processes conform to
the environmental regulations of the country of origin

To find out more about our authors and books visit
www.bloomsbury.com and sign up for our newsletters

'When a single boy underachieves in his exams, it is a failure of the individual. When a million boys underachieve in their exams, it is a failure of policy.'

Ally Fogg (2018)

Contents

Introduction 1

Part 1 **Putting boys' achievement on the agenda** 5

  1 My school days 7

  2 Gender on the agenda 11

  3 Boys will be... 17

  4 Reaching out to parents 25

  5 You would have thought I'd have got it sorted out by now 37

Part 2 **What boys *really* think about...** 45

  6 What makes a good teacher 47

  7 Getting rewards 55

  8 Punishments 63

  9 Peer pressure 71

  10 Academic setting 77

  11 Seating plans 83

  12 How teachers talk to boys and girls 87

13 Single-sex grouping 91

14 Homework 95

15 Reflection 101

16 Writing 105

17 Reading 117

18 What makes a good lesson 125

19 What can help 129

20 What doesn't help and what gets in the way 135

Part 3 Bringing it all together 139

21 The problem with the problem with boys: getting teachers on board 141

22 Be the change you'd like to see 145

23 Street culture 149

24 Pupil voice 153

25 Turning things around 163

26 Mentoring boys: the Breakthrough way 167

27 Raising boys' achievement in an inner London school: a case study 175

References 181
Index 183

Introduction

A freedom of information request to the Department for Education in 2015 asked what policies or initiatives the department had undertaken specifically to address the underachievement of boys. The short answer was this: 'The Department for Education does not fund any initiatives that specifically focus on the underachievement of boys.' Given this complete lack of interest and attention from those at the very top, I propose that we ask the real experts: the boys.

Writing a book like this was tricky because I don't want people hanging onto my words; I want them to hang onto the words of the boys – the real experts. It is well documented that across the entire developed world most girls continue to outperform most boys at every stage of education and (in the UK) in all subjects with the exception of maths at Key Stages 2 and 4. Not all boys underachieve, of course, but of those who are underachieving, at the bottom of the heap are white, working-class boys. My experience of working on the issue of raising boys' achievement since 1993 is that it is a crime that it is not on the national agenda. And why isn't it? Is it precisely because it is working-class boys who are most affected and they don't matter in the scheme of things? Or is it because people are concerned that if we focus on the boys then that will mean the girls will suffer? I call the former a distinct possibility and I call the latter sloppy thinking.

Anything that we do that looks at the behaviour, attitude and performance of boys is bound to have a positive knock-on effect for girls because it can be boys sometimes who behave in ways that are detrimental to everybody's learning. In addition, in all of the books that I have written on the subject, I present strategies that hit all of the buttons for boys without disadvantaging girls. And moreover, if all schools are helping to turn out decent young men, then that surely is also to the benefit of all. It is defined in the title of my first book: *Breaking Through Barriers to Boys' Achievement: Developing a caring masculinity*.

For anyone who is still unsure, can I make the point that there are two areas where boys are massively in the lead? One: 76 per cent of young people who are permanently excluded from school are boys (Department for Education, 2020), and two: in 2019, 96 per cent of the prison population was male (House of Commons Library, 2020). I don't know what that does to anybody else but what it does for me is to get me out of bed first thing in the morning because that's what this work is all about. If our boys do become disaffected or do become disengaged, there is a well-worn path ready and waiting for them and that's the last thing they need. Yes, we know that for men and women there are countless examples of inequalities, so our query might be: do we really need to do things for boys? After all, they're probably going to end up in the top jobs anyway, and if they end up in the same top job as a woman, they may well get 30 per cent more salary. The first thing I'd say in response to this is that the boys we are discussing are far too rarely scaling the heights towards those jobs. The second thing I'd say is that we know such iniquitous situations exist, and that's because we live in a sexist society. There's only one way to change it and that's through education, and it's why many of us came into education in the first place. Developing a caring masculinity can go some way towards combating sexism and making things better for everyone: boys and girls.

This book is not an academic treatise but rather an account of a journey beginning with my own school days as a white, working-class boy who left school without qualifications. This was a journey that continued as a teacher working with countless working-class boys in a number of challenging schools in West Yorkshire for almost 30 years, culminating in life as a consultant with the single aim of engaging schools, local authorities and the government in raising the achievement of these boys, turning them into decent young men and giving them the words to help them unclench their hearts.

So, I begin **Part 1** of the book by telling my own story of the challenges I faced in school, and how I later became a teacher and started to work on the issue of raising boys' achievement at a local and then national level. You'll discover some of the techniques I used to put this issue on the agenda and to start doing things better for boys. I then invite you to do the same thing in your school, through analysing what works and what doesn't work for your male pupils, the barriers they face when it comes to achievement, and crucially, how to *listen* to the boys themselves in order to determine an action plan for improving their experiences of education.

Part 2 of the book considers 15 specific aspects of life in secondary schools from the perspectives of the boys themselves, from what makes a good teacher, to rewards, academic setting, peer pressure, homework and more. You'll hear what boys *really* think about these issues – what helps, what hinders and what we can do to raise their achievement and improve their experiences of school.

Part 3 of the book brings everything together. It raises some further issues for consideration when focusing on boys' achievement, such as getting all teachers on board and the influence of street culture, social media and mental health. I explore in depth ideas for how to run pupil voice projects and group mentoring to successfully listen to the boys in your own school about what matters to them and how to improve your provision in ways that will make a difference. The book concludes with a case study of an inner London school, in which I helped to turn things around for boys.

Throughout the book, you will find the following features that I hope will help you to reflect on your provision for boys, what you are already doing well and what could be improved, and help you put what you are reading into action:

- **What I'd like to see:** Short quotes from boys I have spoken to across my career about changes they'd like to see in their school. These quotes aim to inspire you to think about raising boys' achievement from the perspective of the boys themselves and to focus on doing things differently in your setting.
- **Think:** Reflective questions to encourage you to think more deeply about the issues raised and what this means for your own teaching. Use these to develop your thinking or stimulate discussion with colleagues.
- **Act:** Action points for you to complete in your school to put the suggestions I make into practice.
- **Practical exercise:** More complex, long-term projects you can undertake to listen to the boys in your school and bring about change. These are best completed at a department or whole-school level.

I hope the chapters that follow will help you to think more deeply about boys' achievement in your school and make a difference.

Part 1

Putting boys' achievement on the agenda

Chapter 1

My school days

> **Overview**
>
> - A working-class boy goes to grammar school
> - Teacher training college
> - My first job in teaching
> - Trying to make a difference for boys

As the only boy from the estate to pass the 11-plus and get to a particularly good state grammar school in my village, I was bullied at school for being from the estate and I was bullied on the estate for wearing a grammar school uniform. I also had the experience of being bullied by a PE teacher who, for example, when presented with a note from my mum to say that I had bad hay fever and asthma, would sit me in the long grass to watch cricket instead of play. Incidentally, with regard to the latter, I'm on a mission, and I mention it every day: 'Please take this personally,' I say. Young male PE teachers are undoubtedly the most important male role models a lot of our boys are going to get. See more about this on page 50.

For me, grammar school was a miserable time. It represented one humiliation after another – never anything particularly major, just a steady flow of constant reminders that I was punching above my weight. My first art homework was to redesign a car dashboard. There were no cars in our street. An early project in woodwork was to carve an Easter Island statue out of a bar of soap. It was a real education, but at the same time ultimately depressing. It was an education in so far as I was encountering for the first time the wonderful fragrances of Pears, Palmolive, Lux, Cussons, Camay, Wright's Coal Tar and Imperial Leather. It was depressing as I was the only boy to arrive with what I was (begrudgingly) given by my mother: a half-brick-sized slab of Fairy household soap. It was the only soap that I had ever encountered, a decidedly unsophisticated and rather more industrial product used for scrubbing Dad's collars, cleaning the doorstep, washing up and bath time (but not to wash hair with, oh no, we had Omo or Daz for that).

Art was perhaps the worst, or more specifically, art homework. The rest of my classmates all had beautiful tins of Cumberland or Lakeland crayons with beautiful – to my eyes anyway – metal pencil sharpeners. Pictures were drawn in an array of subtle rainbow colours, but not for me. I developed something of a reputation for colouring my homework using the vast palette of colours that constituted my mother's array of nail varnishes and cosmetics. My homework was always a smudged and scrappy mess, but it smelt sickeningly sweet. Ever since that time, I have been totally in love with beautiful stationery, pens and pencils. Have you visited the pencil museum in the Lake District? I have. Do you know about the green pencils that were manufactured up there for paratroopers during the Second World War? I do. Have you experienced the delights of Palomino pencils, particularly the Palomino Blackwing – 'Half the pressure, twice the speed'? I now have a number of tins of Lakeland crayons. And it doesn't stop there. Only recently did I buy a tin containing a Helix Oxford Maths Set, because I've never owned one, let alone had the opportunity to punch holes in one with a pair of compasses as did all of my peers. Unlike theirs, my tin is in pristine condition. Why wouldn't it be? I have no possible need to use it.

The humiliations were not confined just to me, however. The first session for parents involved meting out humiliation on their heads too. Only days into the first term, all parents were invited to a meeting and all parents were expected to attend. By way of goodness knows what… Was it getting to know each other? Sharing information about the school? I'm not clear, as everything became a blur after the first activity. In a circle, the parents of all 48 new boys had to introduce themselves, give their names and say what they did for a job. And so it began. Lawyer, doctor, solicitor, dentist, lawyer, doctor, company director… spinner, cleaner. Neither my father nor my mother ever returned to the school. I honestly think that their experience of my school was possibly more devastating than mine. Certainly, I'm sure that when I had just finished repeating the fourth form, a totally humiliating experience, they were as relieved as I was when they realised I could now leave school. 'You might as well,' was all they could muster.

Now, I'm not sharing all of this with you for sympathy. I'm perfectly well balanced – I've got a chip on each shoulder. No sympathy required. It was 1967, the 'summer of love'. I was 15. It was the perfect time to drop out of school, grow my hair, wear kaftans and beads, and hitchhike around Europe, sleep in caves in Formentara with hippies from San Francisco, meet countless free spirits and attempt to become a poet or a singer-songwriter. My two best friends at school both went to Cambridge and both got firsts in English. Often I would visit them, experiencing this life that had never been open to me as an option. I remember watching war movies in a popular cinema where the assembled student audience would cheer at the arrival on screen of British soldiers and boo at the sight of the enemy. I remember feeling the part being punted down the river with my shoulder-length hair and white baggy trousers. Five years on, after dabbling in taxi driving, gardening, managing an Indian restaurant, and working as a greengrocer, chauffeur, gravedigger and lots more besides, I was sitting five GCEs as an external candidate at my local tech, without having studied there. You could do that then: for five pounds per subject your local tech would allow you to sit in the same room as 100 or so of their own students and take the exams. I chose art because I could draw, I chose English because I could write, commerce because you only had to read one (very slim) book, general studies because I was told you only needed to read a newspaper for a month and French because I'd had a smattering at school but mostly because of my vast experience of hitchhiking around Europe. That summer, clutching five grade C GCEs, I successfully applied for teacher training college as a (fairly) mature student with a grant (we all got them in those days). Five GCEs were all you needed then. The rest is history. Well to be more accurate, the rest is English and drama.

There were 12 in my group at college, all (reasonably) mature students. For our chosen main subject, English with drama as subsidiary, we studied Sartre, Beckett, Ionescu, Camus, Lawrence, Hardy, Blake, Eliot. For the very first time I discovered the incredible excitement of learning. I couldn't get enough. I became obsessed with Beckett, so much so that I went to Paris one summer break to try and find him in his favourite bar. I stayed there until the very early hours when a knife fight broke out and I skedaddled out of there, only to find myself wandering the backstreets around Les Halles, the meat market no longer in existence, where the gutters then ran with blood.

We had three full terms of teaching practice out of a nine-term course. Unheard of today, but it soon sorted the wheat from the chaff. I spent two full terms under the wing of a remarkable drama teacher, Ray Smith or 'Guttersnipe', as one of his teachers would have it (see page 146). My first full-time job was in a tough, all-boys secondary modern school on the Isle of Thanet on the south coast. It was a school that served the car workers from a nearby car plant that had relocated from East London. To give you a flavour, a small group of boys were expelled the week before Christmas for breaking up milk bottles and encasing the shards in snowballs that they proceeded to hurl at passers-by. As my first year came to a close, I was offered the job of head of English, as I was literally the last man standing in the department. (The only woman working there was the school secretary – oh, and she left too, as it happens.) One of my colleagues left the teaching profession for good after this, his first year. Another left to become a cartoonist. One chose to work for a year in Saudi Arabia and returned to England to buy a house on the strength of it (you could do that in those days). For myself, I heard of a job in the most challenging school in my hometown. I was invited to drop in for a chat with the head who gave me the job there and then (something else you could do in those days). 14 years there and 12 years in an almost equally challenging school constituted my life in classrooms. It was in the latter school that I had the opportunity that I had keenly sought: to try and make a difference for the poor, white, working-class boys I was teaching. I hoped that I could encourage other schools to get this issue on the agenda.

Chapter 2
Gender on the agenda

> **Overview**
> - Why did I start this work in the first place?
> - Establishing a working party: GAWP
> - Hearing it from the girls
> - Doing the research
> - Year 8 is a tricky year for lots of boys
> - The peer police cadets
> - My Top Lads
> - The Pyramid GAWP

'So exactly why did you start the work?' I hear you ask. Well, like all good teachers, I'm going to answer my own question. My interest began in 1993. We had an Ofsted inspection at the school where I was head of English and a senior manager. It was the first year of Ofsted. We were told, and this is going to sound familiar to many, that there was a problem with the way we were delivering collective worship, there was a problem with the plumbing in the science labs and the girls were doing significantly better than the boys, so could we sort it out. I think it was basically the same three issues for the vast majority of secondary schools at the time. What a fabulous use of public money… Inspections cost about £25,000 per school at the time, I seem to remember. Anyway, we set to it. Some things take longer than others, of course: as you know it can take a long time to get a plumber. On day one I was identified as the person to take the lead on the boys question and simultaneously absolve the rest of the staff of any responsibility to help with gender and achievement issues. 'Gary's in charge of boys' stuff.' So, within weeks, I did what all good schools did at the time: I formed a working party. We had several at the time. 'Literacy across the curriculum' was amongst the most popular, I recall. As young English teachers, we used to mock the notion and refer to vomiting and limping across the curriculum. Some still refer to it to this very day (literacy across the curriculum, that is).

I called this brand-new shiny beast of a working party the Gender and Achievement Working Party, which was a bit of a mistake as the acronym (have you worked it out?) is GAWP. Now, to gawp at something where I come from, and it may be the same for you too, means to sit and stare at something for a long time without doing anything about it. It's like, 'What are you gawping at?' And that's exactly how it felt. We spent a long time looking at it, looking into it, looking all over.

Starting with the girls

First on the agenda for the initial GAWP meeting was: 'What about the girls?'. In preparation for the meeting, I began by asking a group of Year 11 girls if they wouldn't mind exploring the issues around boys' achievement in an hour-long meeting. First and foremost, I wanted their honest opinion about starting a project on raising boys' achievement and developing a more caring masculinity. I was keen to let them know that we, as a staff, were clear in our own minds that anything we did related to the behaviour, attitude and performance of boys would be bound to have a positive knock-on effect for girls, as it was obvious that it was more often than not the boys who behaved in a way that would have a detrimental effect on everybody's learning. There was a genuinely positive response. The rest of the meeting concerned itself with how we could help boys achieve as well as girls, and behave as well as they generally did. They got straight to the heart of the issue as it impacted on them. It felt almost as if they'd just been waiting around for someone to ask them.

What I'd like to see

'Well I think boys would do better if they weren't always pestering us in the corridor.'
'Yeah, if they weren't always showing off in front of us in lessons.'
'And behaving immaturely whenever we are around.'

Following on from that, we did lots of work on challenging the macho culture within the school in PSHCE (although it wasn't called that then – I think it was just PS – they've kept adding a new letter every now and then, haven't they?). We developed a sexual harassment policy, which we had published in school planners, on posters, and so on.

We asked the girls lots more things too, such as: 'How can we encourage boys to read as much as girls?' 'Why not create an area of the library that would appeal to them?' came the useful reply. So we did. We created a space and called it the 'Boyzone'. (That was before Boyzone were invented, so I think they owe us some money!)

Above all, we wanted girls to fully understand that, whilst it might seem that the project we were starting was exclusively for the boys, that was certainly not the case. We made it clear that addressing the issues around the prevailing macho culture within the school and hopefully developing a more caring masculinity would be to the benefit of everyone.

Act

Have the discussion with a group of Year 11 girls about the work you are doing or are about to do. Explore their feelings about the project and their ideas to help make a difference.

GAWP marches on

We looked at lots of research. Far too much, to be honest. We discovered, for example, that there was a piece of research in America that seemed to suggest that girls have got superior listening skills in the womb... Yes, I know. Another piece of work suggested that whilst baby girls will smile at smiling faces in the cot, baby boys will smile at balloons. You can try that at home, if you like. We were also told 'if a baby girl is given the kind of toy that she likes, like a doll, she will make up a story with it, and if you give a boy the kind of toy that he likes, like a car, he will just drag the car up his arm and go brrrrmmmmm'. Whether this research had any basis or not, it did at least make us think, 'Mmm. Maybe leaving it until Year 11 is a little bit too late then.' That's exactly what we'd been doing up to that point: taking a group of boys on the borderline (then the grade C or D borderline), or BOBs as somebody unkindly called them, and starting to mentor them at the beginning of Year 11. 'Come on lads,' we'd say, arms around their shoulders, 'Come on lads, you can do it.' Far too little too late. I decided we needed to start lower down the school. The year I chose? Year 8. I've always believed that Year 8 can be a tricky year for lots of boys.

Think

Is this your experience too? Are you doing anything that you feel helps Year 8 boys? Do you have any thoughts on what you might do to give the year more of a focus?

I find Year 7s are very much tied up with transition and settling in; Year 9 is very much to do with options and, at the time of writing, the beginning of GCSEs for many; and Years 10 and 11 are fully focused on GCSEs. Year 8 is a year in which a significant number of boys can start to orientate themselves away from education, often because they come under the cosh of the people I call the peer police (see page 73). Peer pressure. It starts in the nursery: 'You can't wear that. You're a boy and that's pink! What are you playing at?' By the time they get to Year 6, they are starting to drag other boys off cliffs. In virtually every single primary school in the land (if you don't believe me, just ask) there is a small group of boys who are trying to drag other boys off cliffs. I call them the peer police cadets.

My Top Lads

Going back to my own school, throughout Year 7, I kept a careful eye on the group of boys who had been identified as the peer police cadets from the Year 6 classes in our main feeder primaries. Then, in the first week of their second year at the secondary school, I gathered them all up for a lunchtime meeting. You could tell from their faces as they came in that they assumed they were in trouble, or that I was about to announce that they were all stupid and that they were assigned to litter-picking duty. In a similar vein, a primary teacher friend of mine once told me she saw a boy messing about down the corridor, but when she leaned out of her door and shouted, 'You stupid boy!', 20 boys all turned round, assuming it was them. It was a shock to the system then when I immediately announced to them that from that moment onwards they were going to be known as my 'Top Lads' and that they would be working with me for 90 minutes every Friday morning (I wangled extra tutorial time). To this end, we would visit local nursery and reception classes together to help out with reading on a fairly regular basis. They loved it. They loved the fact that they had been given the responsibility of improving or consolidating the school's relations with our main feeder primaries. One boy told me long after the event, 'I was really made up that my little sister saw me round her school doing something so important.' That revelation alone was enough to persuade me to repeat and consolidate the work.

One of my Top Lads even said, 'Before working in nursery and reception, I used to think my little brother and sister were like nothing sorta thing. But since I've been working with the little ones, I've begun to think I need to look after my little brother and sister more.' A few of the other boys told me that as a result of our visits they had started to read to their own little brothers and sisters. Result!

A small group of my Top Lads put together a piece of drama all about bullying with some Year 4s from one school. They travelled around to perform this at other schools. Another group performed street dance in many of our schools. Then there was that brilliant day when we all went down to one of our local infant schools and they taught all the little ones how to make pancakes. Can you see what I was doing? I wasn't just sending the big boys down to the primary schools to coach football or basketball, which is nice. I was challenging some of those old stereotypes and I was giving them a chance to succeed away from the prying eyes of their peers. Also, by giving them a positive focus for their natural leadership ability (the clue's in the title: they're 'peer leaders'), I was giving them the opportunity to turn themselves around. I was very proud of my Top Lads who, by the end of Year 9, were totally disinclined to become a peer police force, but rather a force for good. It really can and does work.

> **Act**
>
> Begin cross-phase buddy reading if not already in place. With those big boys reading to the little ones, that's more than literacy… It's emotional literacy… Big boys, men: they do that stuff as well.

And don't stop with reading! The same principle works in other subjects too, such as maths and science.

> **Act**
>
> For those boys in Year 9 who are doing just about OK in maths but who could do with a boost to their confidence, working as maths ambassadors with the little ones can be transformative for both parties. And what about Year 10 boys doing scientific experiments with Year 5s (not on them… with them!) as science ambassadors?

Finally, have you still got work experience? If so, does it tend to be mostly girls who go down to your partner primary schools? I always encourage secondary schools to send down some of those decent young men as well as the girls – not instead of but as well as. Not least because those little boys really look up to the big boys and it might even encourage a few more men into the teaching profession!

> **Act**
>
> Have that conversation with your partner primaries around work experience and establish the principle of boys and girls visiting on work experience as a regular feature.

The Pyramid GAWP

In these ways, we significantly boosted the connection between ourselves and our feeder primary schools. In those days, we used to call them 'pyramids' of schools, but it never felt right – a secondary school looking down at all of the primaries. Outmoded, and rightly so, it was a very old-fashioned view (although some people still point at aeroplanes where I come from). However, as a group, we very quickly realised that our work with boys needed to be started not at the beginning of secondary school, not even at the beginning of primary school, but from the moment a child started school. It was to that end that we established a Pyramid GAWP! The Pyramid GAWP met on a half-termly basis to discuss strategies such as secondary school boys writing stories for four- and five-year-olds, or teaching playground games and chess (see page 72 for more examples), and projects that involved children in the secondary school and primaries working together in addition to the work of my Top Lads.

> **Think**
>
> Aside from the examples above, are there any other opportunities in your subject area or as a whole school that could have a positive impact for your boys and for the younger ones in your partner primaries?

To cut a long story short, we made a difference. In 1993, the gender gap across the country at GCSE was 8.5 per cent. In other words, 8.5 per cent more girls than boys were achieving five A* to C grades. At the time of writing, converting the number system back to old school grades, the gender gap is almost exactly the same. At my school, in the early nineties, the gender gap was more than double the national average at 18 per cent. We reduced it down to two per cent after two years, and that wasn't to the detriment of the girls – it was by doing the kinds of things that I talk about and write about. The government noticed, as they sometimes do, and I was asked to produce a book entitled *Using Boys' Achievement to Achieve the National Healthy School Standard* for every school in the land. They sent one to every school in 1995. I'm sure lots of you read it. You might remember the blue cover.

Chapter 3
Boys will be...

> **Overview**
> - 'We'd like you to raise boys' achievement across the authority. It's February now; you've got until May.'
> - 'I'm from the local authority. Could you please remove that shirt?'
> - Negative labelling of boys
> - Boys will be brilliant!
> - Labels stick – but it works both ways

The local authority got very excited about my work and invited me into the hallowed halls of power, whereupon they made their proposal. They were keen to second me for a year to, and I quote, 'raise the levels of boys' achievement across the authority at Key Stages 1, 2, 3 and 4. (Pause) It's February now; you've got until May.' And it was just me. 125 primary schools and 26 secondary schools, and it was just me. I took a glance at their smiling faces and the badge that I had been handed that identified me as Gary Wilson: School Improvement Officer. I nodded, shook hands and walked out of the room.

Now, dear reader, do you know Huddersfield at all? No? Do you know we were in the Premier League recently? (Well, fairly recently.) Well, let me describe the scene. In the middle of Huddersfield there is a beautiful library. Next to this beautiful library is this gorgeous piazza, and overlooking this gorgeous piazza used to be (until quite recently) a large department store. Picture the scene. I walk out of the office in the middle of town in a bit of a daze, wondering just what I have let myself in for. I drift past the library… across the beautiful piazza and I look up and there, beaming its message out across the piazza to the entire populace, is a poster, eight foot high, of a boy wearing a red T-shirt emblazoned with the legend, 'I'M LAZY AND I'M PROUD'. I don't know what your reaction would have been, but mine was quite dramatic. I marched into the shop, clutching my local authority name badge, walked over to the young assistant and, brandishing said badge (it was a bit like a scene from *Hawaii Five-0* for anyone who may remember), and said, calmly, 'Excuse me, I'm from the local education authority. Would you mind removing that shirt from your window?'

She looked completely blank (a bit like some of you are now) and uttered tremulously, 'But... I'm er, I'm not the manager.'

'I'll wait,' I said, crossing my arms, to stress the seriousness of this crime against humanity (or the section of humanity that is underachieving boys) and my intent to stay put, until the aforementioned manager appeared. I didn't have to wait too long. Then I struck the closest I could manage to a formidable pose.

'Yes sir, can I help you?'

'It's about this shirt.'

'Yes sir, it's good, innit?' He grinned in the direction of the window display.

'No, it's not good... It's terrible. I work for the local authority, I'm in charge of raising levels of achievement, motivation, aspirations and self-esteem in schools, particularly among boys. Could you please take it down?'

At which point, after a pause, he summoned up a reply, 'I'm afraid I can't do that, sir. It's the new spring collection. It's up for three months.' He paused.

'In that case, can I have the number for head office please?'

So, I rang head office and they put me through to someone in customer relations. I told her the story. She said, 'Well, I can mention it at our senior management meeting.'

I said, 'When's that?'

'Tomorrow morning.'

So, I rang back 'tomorrow afternoon'. 'It's not good,' she uttered meekly.

'Sorry?'

'It's not good,' she repeated. 'It's in 186 high streets across the country and Sir [Doo Dah], the CEO, he thinks this is just a bit of fun on the part of one of his buyers.'

They refused to be moved. But I wouldn't let it lie. To begin with, I thought it was a racist image, as it happened to be a young man of mixed heritage. The head of the CRE agreed and he suggested trying the Advertising Standards Authority. They said there was nothing they could do about things in shop windows. Top tip: you can put anything you like in shop windows and nobody can do anything about it. So, I then contacted my local MP, Chair of the Education Select Committee, and another education minister. I don't know what they did but it was down within a week instead of three months.

Now I mention this every day (sometimes twice) for three reasons. One, because I'm proud of it and I'm showing off. Two, because it gave me lots of positive ideas for schools across my local authority and other local authorities across the country. Three, because it's about the profusion of negative images and messages around boys. Don't our boys get a bad press on this kind of sloganeering? 'He's a boy, what do you expect?'

Boys will be...

Did your brain predict what was coming next? The negative labelling of boys is everywhere. It's on their clothing, from 'Boys are stupid, throw rocks at them' to 'I'm lazy and I'm proud'. One large supermarket chain, only a few years ago, had a section of clothes for girls and there was a big banner above bearing the legend 'Butter wouldn't melt'. The section of clothes for boys had a banner proclaiming 'Here comes trouble'. You can still get a T-shirt bearing the legend, 'Here comes trouble', but they came up with something even better recently: 'Daddy taught me everything I know; it didn't take long'. Double whammy! Only a couple of years ago, in the window of one of the very largest clothing chains during the summer holidays, when they were promoting school clothes for the autumn term, all the little girl mannequins were dressed immaculately. All the little boy mannequins had their ties screwed up and loose and their shirts hanging out of their trousers. It was part of the instructions to all of the company's window dressers the length and breadth of the UK. I know because I asked. It didn't happen the following year. Another large chain, now closed, had a range of clothes for girls called 'Sweet Millie' and a range of clothes for boys called 'Scruff'. Just when you think there are rather fewer of these messages around, up pops something else. A major clothing retailer advertised school wear recently for primary-aged children thus:

Girls' shoes: 'Walk this way for footwear that'll make sure she's a step ahead in class.'

Boys' shoes: 'Walk, don't run! In school shoe styles made to rule the playground.'

Awful? Try this:

Boys' coats: 'Start the new term with a stylish new coat that'll survive playground rough and tumble.'

Girls' coats: 'Turn the playground into a runway with our range of girls' outerwear. Guaranteed to turn heads.' (!!!!!)

Just notice the number of television adverts that make men look useless and pathetic. When are people going to understand that the more negative labels we create around boys, the worse it gets?

One primary headteacher once heard me ranting on about this and when she got home she took one look at the way she'd sent her two children to school that day – she sent me a picture of her little girl sporting a 'Little Princess' T-shirt and her son resplendent in a 'Lazy Bones' sweatshirt. She took one look and then ceremoniously burned them (that's the T-shirts, not the children – don't be alarmed!). Every Early Years practitioner I have ever spoken to has had countless experiences of little boys being handed over on the first day with: 'You'll have your hands full with this one – he's a right little mischief' or 'Well, he's a lad, what do you expect?' and the ever present 'Boys will be boys.'

Our boys don't half get a raw deal, labelled negatively not just on their clothing but also in the press, in the street, in the home… Never mind, 'boys will be boys'. 'Boys will be… BRILLIANT!' From now on, please promise yourself that you'll never ever let the phrase 'boys will be boys' leave your lips again. And what's more, if you catch somebody about to say it, stop them too.

Never mind 'boys will be boys', boys will be BRILLIANT!

Your boys will be brilliant: your boys at home, they will be brilliant because you support them in their education. Close parental involvement in a child's education can significantly raise their levels of achievement. A father's involvement in a boy's education, whether dad lives at home or not, will – we are told – have a significant impact on their future academic success, success in developing relationships and avoidance of criminal activities. Your boys will be brilliant because you believe in them and they know you do. Your boys will be brilliant because you're helping them to develop belief in themselves too. You are helping them develop self-confidence, self-esteem and aspirations. And perhaps above all, your boys will be brilliant because you give them that little extra bit of love just when you know they need it. But the thing is, given the same set of circumstances, *all* boys could be brilliant.

However, because the negative labelling of boys is so all-pervading, it means that sometimes, even as professionals, we can get drawn into it too. I know that it can hurt to realise that this is the case because the bottom line is we love teaching boys – we certainly wouldn't want to do them any harm. We love to see how enthusiastic they get when we grab them with something that interests them. We love the fact they love taking risks. We love the fact that they can be a little bit more challenging sometimes, as that can make it more rewarding. We love their openness, their honesty. We love their sense of fun, their sense of humour, the fun we can have. And perhaps above all, we love the fact that every day's a new day for them. But isn't it a shame it's not always the same the other way round? (Never mind every day – every hour. Many of us know this from our own personal relationships: 'That stuff? That stuff's over with now… isn't it?')

Act

What is it that you like about working with boys? Make a list. Have you commented to your boys on any of these positives recently? If not, give them some praise.

Labels stick – but it works both ways

In countless conversations with countless boys (and grown men) over the 25 years I've been working on boys' achievement, it is very clear that yes indeed, these labels stick. BUT, and it's a significant but, it works both ways. When I was nine, a teacher told me I could write poems and I've been writing poems ever since. Every working day I ask groups of teachers if any of them, in their time at primary school, were ever told to stand up, in turn, to sing a few notes, and if the teacher thought they could sing they would tell them, 'You can sing, you're in the choir,' and if they couldn't sing they were told, 'You can't sing, you can sit down' or 'Stand at the back and mime.' There is usually at least ten per cent in each group who fell into the latter category. Then I ask them if they sing now. Almost every single person says no. On one occasion a primary head bravely described a moment of humiliation that occurred whilst she was taking an assembly. The assembly she had planned included bravely (for her!) singing a nursery rhyme. Only a few lines in, the deputy headteacher interrupted the performance with the words, 'Right children, now I think we know a different tune to this nursery rhyme, don't we?' The deputy headteacher then proceeded to deliver the nursery rhyme note-perfect and with gusto. One teacher once told me, 'I don't even sing at my children's own birthday parties.'

I was working in a secondary school in the UK, and part of the plan for the day was to talk to a group of 15 Years 10 and 11 boys. They duly appeared at the door, sheepish and miserable, herded in by a teacher who couldn't wait to get out of the way after delivery was made. 'Would you like me to stay?' He was out of the door and halfway down the corridor whilst I was still thinking of a reply. I watched as the boys shuffled across the floor, heads bowed, to join me around the conference room table. A big, round table with nowhere to hide. The boy at the front of this unhappy band muttered as he walked past, 'We're the 15 worst boys in school, sir.' Being used to boys assuming the worst when they are removed from classes for meetings with me, i.e. that they were in trouble or they were stupid, I responded with 'Don't be silly, boys.' Whilst smiling benignly, I added, 'What on earth gave you that idea?'

'The principal, sir. He just told us.'

Dumbfounded, not to mention seething, I quickly proclaimed, 'Then maybe we need to get a message back to the principal. Tell me, what has been the problem?'

During the course of that next hour and during the course of many, many more hours, I heard stories from so many boys who felt they had a reputation and they just couldn't shift it. They'd gone into a brand-new class or a brand-new subject or even a brand-new school with a brand-new teacher and the teacher had said, 'I know about you, son. You can sit over there!' Sometimes they didn't even have to say anything. Sometimes it was based on the fact that they happened to share the same surname with someone who had previously been a bother: 'Oh no, not another Cunningham!' (Apologies to any Cunninghams reading.)

> **Think**
>
> Do we listen to ourselves sometimes? 'The teachers all know that my mum's a teacher,' a boy told me, 'and if I put one foot wrong, they're always saying something like, "What *would* your mother say?!"' At a parents' evening as a parent, have you ever heard the dreaded, 'Mmm, he's not like his sister, is he?' Boys particularly hate this – it's not rocket science, is it? Or maybe you've heard a teacher say jauntily, 'Come on, trouble, sit down.' What if the parent challenged this? Parent: 'Is my son trouble?' Teacher: 'Well, err... no.' Parent: 'Then please don't call him that.' Stony silence.

In this particular school, I told the teachers about what the boys had said about their labels and one teacher, Martin, suddenly burst out with, 'You know, I'll never forget my first day at school, four years old... We walked in and in front of each of us was a large piece of paper and a few pots of different-coloured stuff and brush things. I'd never seen anything like it and I'd no idea what to do, but I was very drawn to the red. So, I painted every square inch bright red and then I sat back to admire it. Then the teacher came round and held up a bit of a lopsided house that another child had drawn. "Ooh, what a lovely house, look everybody!" she chirruped. To a sparse-looking tree, she purred, "Ooh, what a lovely tree, Lucy!" Then to a face with one or two limbs sticking out here and there, "What a lurvely face." Then she turned to me. Then she turned to the paper, then back to me, and said, without the singsong voice, "Martin, you're going to be no better than your father... the decorator." I just slumped,' said Martin. 'I just slumped mentally and physically at the age of four.' Martin then proceeded to tell us: 'Two years later a supply teacher came in and showed us how to do 3D drawings and I did a picture of a kennel, which the teacher held up as a good example.'

The thing is, these labels stick, but they work both ways. It's little wonder then that high on a list of what boys think makes a good teacher is someone who gives them a fresh start every lesson. After all, when asked about what they like about teaching boys, teachers often say they love the fact that every day's a new day for them. Isn't it a shame that it's not always the same the other way round?

Hands up if you've ever heard a mood hoover or a lemon sucker in the staff room declare to an anxious supply teacher, 'That lot'll lead you a merry dance' or, along with the mention of a poor boy's name, 'You're going to have to get that one onside' and afterwards, to the same, now frazzled, teacher, 'Well, what did you expect from that lot?' It's OK, you can all put your hands down now. Perish the thought you ever want to reward them for buckling down, doing their best, shaking off that label and turning themselves around. I've heard teachers say, 'You're taking them *where* for an end-of-term treat? I wouldn't take that lot to the end of the street.' Boys know about this stuff. One boy said to me, accompanied by significant numbers of nods around the discussion group: 'I don't like it that teachers who don't know you know your name.' 'Yeah, it's because they all slag you off in the staff room.'

What I'd like to see

'I think teachers should make up their minds about you once they've met you, not before.'

Practical exercise

Who was that inspirational teacher in your life? It might have been someone who taught you or possibly even someone you saw teach at the beginning of your professional career. What was it about them or the thing(s) they said that made them inspirational? How has this affected you in later life? Watch this video of ex-footballer Ian Wright being reunited with his former PE teacher: www.youtube.com/watch?v=eKTolrezxPw and listen to Ian talking about it on BBC Radio 4: www.bbc.co.uk/news/av/uk-51516452/ian-wright-tearfully-remembers-childhood-teacher.

You could have this as an informal item on your department meeting agenda under 'inspirational teachers' or 'Inspirational moments'. Have you ever said anything to one of your pupils that you know has had a powerful positive impact on them? Share these positive moments with your colleagues.

Chapter 4
Reaching out to parents

> **Overview**
> - What can happen when parents get on board?
> - Explaining the issues and what we are doing as a school
> - The impact we can have
> - Advising parents about technology use
> - Developing dialogue at home

At this point, in my own school, with a group of staff on board, I was happily GAWP-ing along in the secondary school, then GAWP-ing with our partner primary schools. We'd also started lower down the school with my Top Lads from Year 8, who worked in our partner primaries. However, I still thought that there was one group missing if we were going to further maximise the impact, and that was parents.

Parents' sessions

The first session I delivered for parents on the subject of boys' achievement was in the autumn term of 1993. 17 mums and five dads turned up. (I know, it's getting better now but not much!) It was no great surprise though, as I recall on so many occasions whenever I would phone home to talk about a boy or a girl, if their dad answered the phone, very often there would be a short pause and then, 'I'll just go and get her.' I presume the assumption was that it's education and that's what mums do. By the way, at that first parents' session, a lot of mums were saying they were still packing their boy's bag at the age of 15. And it doesn't seem to matter whether it's a secondary headteachers' conference, an INSET day or a twilight session: whenever I mention it, a frisson of guilt goes around the room and one or two of the men stare at their shoes and you see them think, 'Actually, my wife packed my bag this morning. Does it matter?'

I continue to deliver parents' sessions to this day. What typifies most parents' sessions in my experience is that the parents that you really want to see are the ones who never come. I consider myself to be very fortunate, therefore, to have been asked by a small group of parents after that very first meeting if there was any way they could help get the messages across to all parents. I suggested that maybe they'd like to form a working group and, with my help, produce a leaflet of information for all parents to help them help their boys. The leaflet contained reference to the importance of, for example:

- ✓ giving lots of encouragement to boost confidence
- ✓ giving him more responsibilities around the house
- ✓ not doing everything for him
- ✓ encouraging a reading habit
- ✓ creating opportunities at home for learning
- ✓ limiting leisure time spent in front of screens (good luck – this was 1993! I think it was just two white lines with a bouncing ball going 'Ping!' in those days!)
- ✓ talking to his teacher if you have concerns
- ✓ guiding him towards out-of-school activities which he will enjoy but also at which he can succeed (lots of mums were saying that his dad takes him to play football on a Sunday morning and the poor lad is the permanent reserve; he's standing there on the touchline on a weekly basis and his self-esteem and confidence are slowly sinking into the ground. I know: I was one of those dads and I have to live with it every time I mention it. Leave me alone!)

And, above all:

- ✓ persuading him that talking over problems is best, as it can help release tension and anger
- ✓ reassuring him that it's OK to express his feelings – in fact, positively encourage it.

It was helpful, I believe, because it was parents sharing advice with other parents. It wasn't the government, the local authority or the school that was doing it. (The full leaflet can be found in *Breaking Through Barriers to Boys' Achievement* should you wish to see it.)

The leaflet was ultimately used by schools right across the authority for a number of years at new intake evenings in both primary and secondary schools. I believe there's nothing wrong with spending ten minutes at such an evening to say:

'Most of you will have heard that there is a disparity between boys' and girls' examination results. Every summer the headlines ring out "Girls outperform boys at GCSEs yet again" or some such. And yet nobody takes the trouble to explain why

this keeps on happening. Few stand up and make the point that this isn't just a school issue, a local issue or even a national issue – it happens all over the developed world. However, as a school we are aware of the problem and we are working hard to ensure that all of our students succeed, by, for example, seeking out and dealing with peer pressure, which is a particularly pernicious form of bullying. If you believe your son is under pressure from other boys simply because he wants to work hard, then school needs to know. We are also looking closely into boys' attitudes towards school, writing, homework, rewards, punishment, and so on. And we will be listening to them. What is particularly important is that parents understand the issue and understand the role that they can play to support their boys.'

Act

Create some materials for the parents of boys in your school as described (or modify the leaflet from *Breaking Through Barriers to Boys' Achievement*). Deliver them at each new intake evening.

Alternatively, if you feel that the new intake evening is a bridge too far, or if indeed you want to address the parents of all boys, and (recommended) you want to invite the parents of all boys in your feeder or partner primary schools, you could:

- hold a parents' session for the parents of all boys, from Years 7 to 11
- invite the parents of boys from your partner primary schools.

We know, from our own experience as teachers, that we are more likely to get parents in good numbers if the invite is given face to face, or by phone or text message. If you are involving a group of boys in a project, it goes without saying that their parents need to be invited. If, like many schools involved in the Breakthrough Project (see Chapter 26), you decide to make an event of this, get the boys to cook and prepare supper. However you choose to run it, you need to get your act together front-of-house-wise too. Forgive me, but this is a real bugbear of mine and it's rather tricky to have to say. But here goes: in my experience of delivering hundreds of parents' sessions in both primary and secondary schools, primary schools beat secondaries hands down on making parents feel welcome, comfortable and more than happy to return to the next event. I have delivered a number of parents' sessions in secondary schools when the headteacher hasn't attended (rare but it does happen), when a solitary deputy has been the only member of staff there (fairly common), and when there have been no refreshments (astonishingly common). And I remember one occasion when I was in a freezing cold dining room, going on about making sure boys' physiological needs are met first and foremost, only for my every word to be virtually drowned out by the low rumble of the Slush Puppie machine. (I have photographic evidence!)

Of course, as secondary teachers, we might argue that the relationship between parents and a child's primary school is very different to the ones we enjoy (or rather, should we say, fail to enjoy) due to the size of the school, the fact there's usually just the one teacher per year, and so on. But these shouldn't be seen as the reasons why secondary schools and parents fail to work happily and productively with each other. Rather we should see that there is all the more reason for secondary schools to reach out to parents more effectively than they do at present. (There, that didn't hurt too much, did it?)

Think

How well does your school welcome parents? Is there any room for improvements to be made? Such as?

Act

We know that the most effective ways of attracting parents to an educational event are invitations given in person or by phone. A letter or text will be helpful but on its own it will have limited impact. Create a plan to engage as many parents as you can and in whatever ways you believe will be effective. You could use this draft letter as a starting point.

HELP YOUR BOYS SUCCEED

Dear parents and carers of boys,

You are probably aware of the fact that boys can often do less well in school than girls. Every year, when examination results are out, the headlines in the newspapers announce that girls outperform boys – yet again. But nobody takes the trouble to explain why. It's not a local problem, or even a national problem. It is an international problem. There are many reasons for it and it's not simple. For example, some boys tend to be rather less independent than girls when they're younger, tend to develop language more slowly than girls, and often read less. A lot of boys tend to spend more time playing computer games than girls, revise less and can be less organised. Not all boys underachieve, as we know, and there are things that we are doing as a school to reduce the gap. We feel as a school that it is also very important that as parents and carers you know exactly what all the issues are, and *what you can do to help support your boys. This is why we are inviting you along to explain the issues in more detail, outline what we're doing as a school and give you some practical ideas of what you can do to help.*

Starting early: out of the mouths of babes

12 years after I'd delivered my first ever parents' session in 1993, I was addressing parents at an infant school in a very poor part of South Yorkshire. Only seven mums turned up that evening... and they brought their sons. I think they thought I was a magician and that I was going to wave a magic wand and their boys would be all right. I talked about all the usual stuff I talk about:

- The importance of men in the close and extended family reading to and with their boys, and not stopping just because their boys can read by themselves. According to the Book Trust (2020), only 37 per cent of children up to the age of nine in the UK are reading with or being read to by a parent or carer for over an hour a week in total, and a significant number are read to only by mums. It may well be that the boy may not have a man at home, but even if he does, he might never be read to by a man, he may never see a man around the house reading, and if he does, he may have only ever seen us reading a newspaper or an instruction manual. Therefore, they think, I'm a boy, and boys only read to find out things.
- The importance of not doing everything for him, but developing and supporting his independence.
- The importance of joining a children's library. I discovered in my own local authority that 75 per cent of under-fives who were members of libraries were girls. What on earth are parents thinking? 'Well, he's a boy, he won't be interested in reading, so I'll not bother.' Or maybe, 'he's going to show us up at the library, so I'm not going to bother.' Whatever it is, it's an issue.
- The importance of sitting around tables and eating and talking together. In many homes, families do not have a table to sit at and talk during mealtimes and many people eat their meals watching screens.

And lots more.

At the end of the session, one parent came up to me (and I'm not mocking her) and said, 'That were really interesting that stuff that you said, Mr Wilson. That stuff you said about libraries and that. Our Marcus...' (our Marcus was swinging on the curtains at the back of the stage at the time), 'our Marcus keeps saying (mimics) "Can I join t' library mam, go on, mam? Can I join t' library? You know, that van that comes round, can I join?" And I've been saying to him, "No, you can't... you bloody well can't." I've been... using it as punishment like.' A heavy silence fell upon us as she stared at me, hoping for a nod or a smile in agreement. There was none. Only a look of total bemusement on my part. 'And that other stuff you were saying about sitting round t' table and eating and talking and that. It's funny that, 'cos we were watching t' telly other night and our Marcus said, "Can't we have us tea round t' table, mam? Go on, mam, can't we have us tea round t' table, like they do on *The Simpsons*?"'

The Simpsons?! Positive role models? Who woulda thunk it? I came away thinking, 'I'm glad I went. For that one mum, that one boy, it'll make a difference.'

Days later I consoled myself with the thought that it was exactly like the story about the starfish: you know, the one about the boy who was gently throwing things into the sea when a passer-by enquired, 'What are you doing?' to which the boy replies, 'The tide is going out and they're stranded on the beach. I can't bear to see them struggle.' The man replied, shaking his head, 'But the beach is miles long. It will hardly make a difference.' At which point, the boy picked up another and replied, gently throwing the starfish back into the water, 'It made a difference to that one.' Yes, I'm glad I went, that one mum, that one boy. But the other thing I thought was, 'Hey, hang on, it's worse than I thought. There are four- and five-year-olds out there who know what's good for them better than their parents do, and unless we get these messages across to parents, it's like writing on that little internal whiteboard every day and every night they go home and it's wiped clean. Writing on that little internal whiteboard every day and so much of what we do is a total waste of time.'

Technology

At parents' sessions in secondary schools there are certain issues that do arouse some interest. In 'any questions' at the end of my sessions, the agenda has shifted from 'How long should he be spending on his homework?' (an old evergreen) and 'How much time is it OK for him to watch TV?' to the gentle enquiry, 'Er... how much time is it appropriate for him to be spending on computer games?' and (on the verge of hysteria), 'How can I get my boy surgically removed from his games console?'

> **Think**
>
> Think about what boys have to say about technology. Are we as teachers presenting a totally negative and biased view on boys and computers? I've heard boys say in the past: 'My parents don't realise that if they take my computer away, they're taking away my social life' and 'If I get into trouble at school, Mum takes my phone off me for a week... I wonder how teachers would feel if that happened to them.'

Parents are worried, and rightly so. What is frustrating to parents is that there is so much conflicting information about the whole issue. In 2017, the NHS declared addiction to computer games to be an area that demanded their resources to help the rehabilitation of young addicts. It is clearly another issue where we need to listen to what the boys have to say. We need to know about the amount of time they spend on computers, whether this affects their sleep patterns, the time it leaves for homework and, at critical times of the year, the impact upon revision and, subsequently, examinations.

In discussion groups with boys, the minute I bring up the subject of the inordinate amounts of time being spent on the latest computer games, all their attention immediately turns to the three or four boys who are well-known for the prodigious amount of time they spend in such employment. It's not unusual to hear from this handful that they head directly to their games console after a cursory look over, and minimal attempt at, homework, followed by a mealtime spent in silence, or at most, a mealtime punctuated by grunts when asked about their day. Common to most is that computer games do take up an enormous amount of time. I've heard boys say, 'I reckon I waste a day a week of my life on computer games' and 'I'm never in bed before 11 and even then I'm on my phone.'

A project I conducted with every 15- and 16-year-old boy in Derbyshire in 2008 highlighted the fact that on average they were spending at least four or five hours a night on computer games, most were going to bed too late and most were having problems getting to sleep. Why? It is well understood that you need to have at least an hour's downtime after being on a computer before you try and sleep, possibly more. The worst thing we can do for our own stress levels, by the way, is to check our emails last thing at night… but we'll still keep doing it though, won't we? What hope have we got with the kids, eh? Add to this the fact that around 70 per cent of the boys weren't bothering with breakfast on a regular basis so what kind of state were they in for learning the next day?

The advice I offer at parents' sessions is: no screens around tables at any time. No computer games on Monday, Tuesday, Wednesday or Thursday, unless they've done something to deserve it: 'You've had a good day at school' or 'You've finished your homework' or 'You've helped me with tea. You can play on the computer for an hour (or an hour and a half).' Draconian? Not quite as bad as a parent who said to me once, 'I've turned off the router to every room in the house apart from the front room, and now the weather's getting colder, I've turned off the heating in every room in the house apart from the front room. We're having a lot more friendlier, calmer, happier family time.' This in turn is certainly not as bad as a well-known TV personality who owned up to smashing her sons' tablets.

> **Act**
>
> Develop guidelines for parents when it comes to managing their child's relationship with technology. If you don't already, you could possibly include department-by-department recommendations for sites that are seen as particularly useful or inspiring.

The overarching message that I believe we need to communicate to parents, and of course to the boys themselves, is that we are not luddites but we want our youngsters to be masters of technology, not slaves to it. Together we would be delighted if we could move them along from being passively engaged with technology to being actively and creatively involved with it. In other words, move them from being browsers, viewers and listeners to being creators of music and film, writers of blogs and ebooks and designers of computer games.

Communication at home

Of course, a significant issue for all parties is that the inordinate amount of time so many boys spend on computer games means there is less social interaction in the home and, in a nutshell, less talk. It is widely understood that girls develop language faster than boys (in other words, it seems that boys have 'weaker' or 'slower' capacities for language acquisition). Boys represent more than 70 per cent of late talkers and just 30 per cent of early talkers (Kovačević, 2006). It is also widely understood that girls tend to be far more capable of talking about their feelings. Boys often have problems putting pen to paper without talking through, debating or arguing their ideas first, all the way through school. Boys need to talk.

However, if you are the parent of a boy, you will probably be aware of the grunt culture. It goes something like this:

Parent: 'What have you done at school today?'

In Early Years, he might have replied, 'I played.'

In primary, 'Nothing.'

In secondary, 'Hrrrumff.'

But then as parents we know how to get to the heart of the boy. It's when we're taking him somewhere in the car. Just you and him… You're here, he's there, he's a prisoner, he can't get out. Perfect! But it's perfect in one particular way, that is, because it's side by side. Try side by side at the sink… Sell the dishwasher! One teacher told me that she always knows when her lad (her lad is 28) has a problem: 'He'll invite himself round for tea and at some point during the meal he'll quietly say, "I'll help you with the washing up, mam." It's his little signal that he wants a quiet word.' Parents know this, but as teachers, we very easily forget. There's a little altercation or a little problem with a boy who is angry and upset, and what do we say? 'Just look at me when I'm talking to you!'

Bonus questions for parents

Instead of the usual 'What did you do in school today?', suggest that parents try the following alternatives to mix it up a bit and help open up the lines of communication with their boys:

- ✓ 'What was the best question you asked at school today?' Einstein's parents used to ask him the same question every single day. Didn't do him any harm did it?
- ✓ 'What was the funniest thing that happened today? What was the funniest thing a teacher said today?'
- ✓ 'What was the one thing you learned today that you'll remember for a long time?'
- ✓ 'Did any teacher praise you today? What was it for? How did it make you feel?'

Don't take no (or silence, or a grunt) for an answer.

Another possible approach is this one that a teacher once reported to me she'd tried in order to engage with her normally reticent son. She used a method of teaching we had discussed with staff. Something I call piggy-back learning. Teaching others what you have just been taught is known to be one of the most powerful ways to retain memory.

On that basis, and armed with that information, upon her son arriving at the tea table, she idly, almost nonchalantly, asked whether or not he'd done his revision – you know the score, she bided her time, used a tone of voice that sounded like she was only mildly interested, waited for an opportune time, midway between pizza and pudding, and put it out there.

'Mmmmm?'

'What's it on?'

'Errr, ratios.'

'Oh… ratios, I don't understand ratios. I never could. Show me.'

'We had an hour together. It was brilliant.'

The assumption that education is largely the mother's province can be very strong in many homes. Of course, when both parents engage in their youngster's learning the benefits do increase.

What does and what doesn't represent positive, supportive engagement can vary significantly from home to home. Schools taking the trouble to alert parents about issues relating to boys' underachievement and giving them the strategies that they might use to support their boys can sometimes be more than simply useful but indeed absolutely vital.

'I really don't know why he's not doing the work for you'

On one occasion, in a school in Northern Ireland, the principal's opening remarks to a parents' session I was delivering were short and to the point: 'I am reminded, Mr Wilson, of an occasion when I once had the need to talk to a parent about her son's homework (or the complete lack thereof). The mother was dumbfounded, "Well, Mr Robinson, I have no idea why he is not doing the work for you. He has all the time in the world at home to do it. I make sure of that. I do everything for him. I take him his breakfast in bed every single day. And (as if she hadn't said or done enough already) I always take his butter up separately as he doesn't like his toast to be soggy."' Here there was a pause from the mother as she pondered her son's misdemeanour and also one from the principal as he contained his incredulity.

For the vast majority of parents, the whole issue around the underachievement of boys is not exactly a mystery, as they see all the negative stereotyping of boys presented by the media, which serves to perpetuate that dreadful 'Well, boys will be boys' syndrome. Schools desperately need to reach out to parents to say, 'Yes, there is an issue with regard, particularly, to white, working-class boys underachieving in relation to girls, and it is not just locally, or nationally, or internationally; it is the same across the entire developed world' (apart from those countries, as we have seen, most notably some Scandinavian countries, where they don't start school until they are six or seven).

Schools need to be very clear in their messages to parents that:

- ✓ They understand the complexity of the issue.
- ✓ They are not prepared to stand by and let any negative stereotyping of boys persist in their school.
- ✓ They are currently working on a range of strategies, such as dealing with peer pressure. (Parents need to know that if their son has been a victim of negative peer pressure then the school should be informed as it considers peer pressure to be a particularly pernicious form of bullying.)
- ✓ There are many contributions they can make to help their boys succeed.

To invite parents in to a meeting to learn more about what a good school like theirs is currently doing and what parents can do to help is a good starting point. But it's important not to just stop there. The following extract from a school's newsletter is a good example of a school being totally transparent about the issue. In addition, it's being very clear about how significant the school believes pupil voice can be.

Rewards and behaviour update for parents

We still have work to do as a college to improve and embed our systems. Thank you to those parents who have given us feedback already. This has led to changes such as our text message system giving parents clearer information and better communication regarding pupil achievement. This means that you can see the subject area, period and member of staff who has rewarded or sanctioned your child.

At the moment there is a 6:1 ratio of rewards to consequences across the college. This confirms our anecdotal evidence that good behaviour is being noticed, students are being encouraged, and disruption to learning is diminishing. So far, over 37,000 rewards have been awarded across the college. There is a fairly even and proportional distribution across year groups; the exception to this seems to be Year 11 who at present have been awarded less. This is something we are addressing with staff to ensure consistency. We are also working to ensure that rewards and sanctions are proportionate to the curriculum time, so that there is consistency across subject areas. Our initial data suggests that there is no significant gender gap when rewards are awarded. Our consequences data does show a significant gender gap, so we are working as a college to address strategies for engaging boys in particular.

One way we have worked to ensure that our systems are appropriate and effective is by holding student conferences to get the views and suggestions of our students. Students asked us to better communicate the reasons for their rewards and consequences. We know that we need to work on changing student perceptions about the college, as despite the positive ratio across year groups, only 45 per cent of students are telling us behaviour has significantly improved. We want to ensure that this percentage is much higher and we need to continue to work together to make that difference.

Practical exercise

Consider what a report about behaviour and rewards might have sounded like from your school. Sketch out an equivalent report. Whether better or worse than the example here, what are the implications for you as a school?

Chapter 5

You would have thought I'd have got it sorted out by now

> **Overview**
> - Why is it not on the national agenda?
> - Reach out and talk to your boys, the real experts
> - What has been attempted before?
> - Why are boys underachieving?
> - Defining the barriers in your school

So, I have now been working on raising boys' achievement at a local and national level for 27 years. You would have thought I'd have got it sorted by now, wouldn't you? But sadly, not many people are doing anything about it. The laudable Homerton Report (Younger et al., 2005) considered raising boys' achievement with strategies in four different areas: pedagogic (classroom-based approaches centred on teaching and learning), individual (target-setting and mentoring), organisational (organising learning at the whole-school level) and socio-cultural (creating an environment where key boys and girls feel able to work with, rather than against, the aims and aspirations of the school). However, since the publication of the Homerton Report, I have heard no government pronouncements about the gender issue at all. I tell a lie: there was one, when a certain, extremely unpopular minister for education stated, 'We're going to reduce the gender gap by making sure more three-year-old boys read more books.' Brilliant! Fingers on the pulse as always.

This is just so wrong in so many ways. As everyone knows, there is only one area in the developed world where boys are achieving as well as girls (and primary teachers are fed up of hearing about it) and that's Scandinavia. And in Scandinavia they don't start school until they're six or seven. Prior to that, they're learning actively, outdoors and largely through play, which is exactly where our boys need to be. This in turn puts an enormous amount of pressure on our Early Years colleagues who are having to work incredibly hard to even begin to get the boys to catch up. In addition, and as if that weren't enough pressure, parents are pressurised to do whatever they can pre-school to help prepare their boys well enough to jump onto that fast-moving train at the age of four. Parents, and dare I even suggest it, middle-class parents, can very often add to the anxiety levels when their boy can't read or write before he starts school. It doesn't matter that he can't read… but it matters that he loves stories. It doesn't matter if he can't write, but it matters that he has got reasonably well-developed fine motor skills.

The issues around the underachievement of boys are not straightforward and they're not going away. It's time for everyone in education to talk to the real experts: the boys themselves. I urge schools to simply talk to their boys, listen to what they have to say and thus be guided by them to a real understanding of how things are for them. As teachers, we can, with their help, reach out and make those changes that might just make that difference for them. It is my dearest wish that this process will subsequently ensure that schools will place the achievement of boys and, in particular, white, working-class boys, firmly on their school improvement agenda.

What has been attempted before?

For many schools, of course, this may not be for the very first time they are considering this. For many, 'the boys' issue' will bring back memories of having attempted to tackle the very same things before in the dim and distant past because yes, it's true, dear reader, there is nothing new in education. The same things just keep coming round time and time again. I once met a headteacher who'd been a head for 20 years and who said to me she'd been at the forefront of educational thinking three times! One example springs to mind: first there was grammar in the literacy strategy at Key Stage 1 and then there wasn't. Then guess what happened? They put it back in again. What if the Hokey Cokey *was* what it's all about, eh? But the trick is to recognise what really works and hang onto it like grim death, then pull it all together with all those other things that work, not least by asking boys what they think about our efforts on their behalf, what it is that works for them and what else we might try.

The following list suggests some of the measures that you might have seen attempted previously.

Think

Have any of the following been attempted in your school in the dim and distant past in order to help reduce the gender gap? Did they leave staff dispirited when they brought about limited success in terms of the difference those or similar efforts made? If that should be the case in your place of work, and very little impact was made, what are your thoughts on the following?

1. **Were the views of boys and girls sought and acted on?** These issues might have been rewards, punishment, what in their opinion makes a good teacher, their feelings about seating and setting, what they find helps them to achieve in certain subjects, what classroom strategies really inspired and engaged them, and generally what was helpful and what might have had a negative impact on their learning. Is this something you might do now?

2. **Was the gender balance explored in terms of representation?** This might have been representation on school councils, in display materials or at presentation evenings. Or perhaps it was involvement in extracurricular activities, library use, or pupils' feelings about male and female teachers.

3. **Were a small number of strategies (such as single-sex grouping or boy–girl seating) implemented and subsequently abandoned?** Perhaps this was due to limited impact.

4. **Was the work begun with Year 11s?** Did you enjoy limited success with some of the cohort but insufficient to make it worth repeating? Do you now feel that that was far too late for many and perhaps you might begin lower down the school, in Years 8 or 9?

5. **Did mentoring break down due to the reliance upon very busy senior leaders in the process?** Could you perhaps develop another approach to mentoring, such as group mentoring or assertive mentoring (see page 169)?

6. **Was there (and is there still) a certain amount of resistance amongst some staff to engage with the boys' issue because they believe it would mean the girls would suffer?** As already highlighted, and what should really drive this agenda, is the fact that we know categorically that anything we do that looks at the attitude, the behaviour and subsequently the performance of boys is bound to have a positive effect on girls. Pointing out the issues raised in this book, can you have that discussion as a staff now?

7. **Has work on the development of the social and emotional aspects of learning been limited in delivery and subsequently impact?** Has it failed to make barely any impact on changing the nature of the school?

8. **Was the responsibility for working on raising the achievement of boys made the responsibility of just one member of staff?** It seems ridiculous reading that back to myself – what, one person in charge of half the school population? No, wait, if you believe, as I most certainly do, that all this work will also have massive benefits for girls, what we are saying here is that that person has been given responsibility for the whole school! This means that many would absolve themselves of the responsibility of doing anything because 'Gary is in charge of boys.'

9. **Did you, as a secondary school, work with partner primaries to help reduce the need to constantly reinvent the wheel?** Perhaps this was with the peer police cadets, for example. And, most importantly, were the areas for attention

prioritised in a systematic fashion at subject, faculty or whole-school level? Can you see how this might be readdressed?

Practical exercise

If *any* of the above reflect your experience, then hold a senior leadership team (SLT) meeting to explore what you have tried in the past to address the issue, focusing on the successes and disappointments and what you might do differently now.

Why are boys underachieving?

Most of us will already have thought at various times about why many boys are doing less well than girls. This reason always comes in the top three: if only there were more male teachers in primary schools, our boys would be all right. My response to that is always, 'Look, it's not going to happen. Get over it. Move on.' We can't absolve ourselves from doing anything for boys while we're waiting for the men to come on board. That's no disrespect to male teachers, but the percentage of the teaching profession that is male and under the age of 30 is now less than four per cent (Department for Education, 2019). So, it's just as well that it's not the gender of the teacher that's the most important thing, rather it's the quality of the teacher. And at the heart of that is how well they can recognise and link into what's going on in a boy's head, a boy's world, a boy's universe. Some people suggest that men might be at an advantage in that respect; other people dare to suggest that maybe female teachers who are the mothers of boys have got an advantage. (I promise I'll keep mentioning parents in this book so long as you promise me a) not to feel guilty and b) to give him a great big hug, whether he wants one or not, and say to him, 'You're doing so well, especially bearing in mind everything I've just been reading!')

Another common conclusion in the debate around boys' underachievement is that it's to do with 'this laddish behaviour that we see a lot of these days'. But of course a lot of laddish behaviour is actually a cry for help. Have you ever seen it that way? As far as a lot of boys are concerned, it's far better for them to be seen not to be bothered about winning than it is to enter and not win.

Then there is the joyous cry of teaching and learning styles – 'I know, I've been on a course!' Well, we will do a quick Shake n' Vac to bring the freshness back. Oops, lots of young teachers out there will have no idea what I'm talking about. This is a chemical we used to sprinkle on our carpets in the old days, then we used to sing and dance as we hoovered it up.

In a nutshell, I've got it down to not just one, two or three reasons why some of our boys are not doing as well as they might. I've got it down to around 30, but I'm still working on it. The grids in the following section contain my list of barriers, with space for you to add any more as you feel necessary. For those revisiting the issue of gender or beginning a scrutiny of the issues, this will hopefully help to focus the mind!

Defining the barriers in your school

All schools differ, so it's important to work out which of these 27 barriers are most prevalent among the boys in your context. Find out what staff think are the main three areas that they feel they need to focus on to raise boys' achievement. Then determine what the boys themselves would like the school to focus on. Finally, ask the boys what the three main areas are that boys need to focus on for themselves. The practical exercises that follow will help you with this. The chapters in Part 2 of the book hone in on many of these specific aspects. Once you've established which of these factors are most common among your pupils, focus on the relevant chapters in Part 2 to help guide you to improve these aspects of your provision and make things better for the boys in your school.

Practical exercise

As a faculty, department, pastoral team or senior leadership team, consider:

1. Which of the following barriers represent an accurate description of the situation as you see it for boys, in your experience?
2. How highly do they feature as a priority? Rank each barrier on a scale of 0 to 5, with 0 being low priority and 5 being high priority.

Barrier impacting on boys' achievement	Priority
1. Lack of independence	5 4 3 2 1 0
2. Hyper-physical break times	5 4 3 2 1 0
3. Poor written presentation	5 4 3 2 1 0
4. Writing often seen as irrelevant and unimportant	5 4 3 2 1 0
5. Difficulties with structuring written work	5 4 3 2 1 0
6. Reticence to spend a lot of time on planning and preparation	5 4 3 2 1 0
7. Reading seen as a female province	5 4 3 2 1 0
8. How we talk to boys and how we talk to girls	5 4 3 2 1 0
9. Teacher expectations	5 4 3 2 1 0
10. The negative labelling of boys	5 4 3 2 1 0
11. Emotional intelligence issues	5 4 3 2 1 0
12. Mismatch of the preferred ways of teaching to boys' preferred ways of learning	5 4 3 2 1 0

Barrier impacting on boys' achievement	Priority
13. Lack of opportunities for reflective work	5 4 3 2 1 0
14. Pupil grouping	5 4 3 2 1 0
15. Inappropriate seating arrangements	5 4 3 2 1 0
16. Ineffective group work	5 4 3 2 1 0
17. Peer pressure	5 4 3 2 1 0
18. Inappropriate reward systems	5 4 3 2 1 0
19. Laddish culture	5 4 3 2 1 0
20. The influence of street culture	5 4 3 2 1 0
21. The lack of positive male role models	5 4 3 2 1 0
22. The use of non-performance enhancing drugs	5 4 3 2 1 0
23. Self-limiting beliefs	5 4 3 2 1 0
24. Lack of engagement with the life of the school	5 4 3 2 1 0
25. Homophobic bullying	5 4 3 2 1 0
26. Lack of parental understanding of boys' issues	5 4 3 2 1 0
27. Intervention arriving too late	5 4 3 2 1 0
28.	5 4 3 2 1 0
29.	5 4 3 2 1 0
30.	5 4 3 2 1 0

Main barriers to boys' achievement as perceived by the _____ department	Ideas for action
1.	
2.	
3.	

Adapted from *Breaking Through Barriers to Boys' Achievement: Developing a caring masculinity* (Wilson, 2013)

At the same time as completing the above exercise as a staff team, ask a carefully selected group of boys in your school to complete a similar table, such as the one below. You can then match up the responses to both exercises and meet in the middle. Ensure that the boys know that their opinions are being sought by the school for a significant piece of research.

Ask the boys to rank each of the following experiences they may have in school on a scale of 0 to 5, with 0 being 'no experience of this' and 5 being 'regular experience of this'. You can leave a space for them to add their own experiences and let you know what they see as the main barriers to their achievement plus their suggestions for action.

School experience	Your rating
1. I remember relying on others doing everything for me when I first started school at four and I still experience this!	5 4 3 2 1 0
2. I do have physical break times.	5 4 3 2 1 0
3. I struggled with writing at first as it hurt my hand and I still do and it still does.	5 4 3 2 1 0
4. I don't see the point in a lot of the writing we're asked to do.	5 4 3 2 1 0
5. I struggle with structuring written work.	5 4 3 2 1 0
6. I don't like to spend time on planning and preparation.	5 4 3 2 1 0
7. I don't spend any time reading for pleasure.	5 4 3 2 1 0
8. I think that teachers talk to boys and girls differently, treat boys and girls differently.	5 4 3 2 1 0
9. I think teachers have lower expectations of boys.	5 4 3 2 1 0
10. I think that some boys are labelled in a negative way and struggle with reputations sometimes.	5 4 3 2 1 0
11. I find it hard to talk about my emotions.	5 4 3 2 1 0
12. I would prefer more practical work in certain lessons.	5 4 3 2 1 0
13. We don't get much chance to check that we've taken in the learning in a lesson.	5 4 3 2 1 0
14. I don't like setting.	5 4 3 2 1 0
15. I would prefer to sit and work with my friends.	5 4 3 2 1 0
16. In group work, I'd like to help decide who should be in the group.	5 4 3 2 1 0
17. I get teased or even bullied because I want to work hard.	5 4 3 2 1 0
18. I don't think our reward system works very well.	5 4 3 2 1 0
19. A lot of boys behave badly.	5 4 3 2 1 0

School experience	Your rating
20. The influence of street culture has a negative effect in school.	5 4 3 2 1 0
21. There are very few positive male role models in today's society.	5 4 3 2 1 0
22. Some boys become involved with soft drugs.	5 4 3 2 1 0
23. A lot of boys lack confidence and belief in themselves.	5 4 3 2 1 0
24. Some boys don't get involved with any extracurricular activities.	5 4 3 2 1 0
25. Homophobic bullying isn't being dealt with.	5 4 3 2 1 0
26. Parents don't understand all the stuff about boys and what they can do to help.	5 4 3 2 1 0
27. It's too late to change things for boys in Year 11.	5 4 3 2 1 0
28. School doesn't seem to be doing things to help boys succeed as well as girls.	5 4 3 2 1 0
29.	5 4 3 2 1 0
30.	5 4 3 2 1 0

Main barriers to boys' achievement as far as I can see	Ideas for action
1.	
2.	
3.	

Part 2

What boys *really* think about...

Chapter 6
What makes a good teacher

> **Overview**
> - Respect and consistency
> - Teachers who are real people
> - Does gender matter?
> - Male PE teachers
> - Good teachers: a checklist – how do you score?
> - Teacher report card

It's sad to relate but more than one boy has described their experience of school as being one where 'it's easier to develop a bad relationship with a teacher here than it is to develop a good relationship'. Boys recognise a good teacher when they see one and they'll tell you exactly what it is that that teacher has done to make them feel that way. Boys also know how important their teacher is to their success. One Year 10 boy, representing the opinion of many boys over the years, said, 'I value my relationship with my teacher. The grade you get is definitely affected by the teacher you have.'

Respect and consistency

One of the most common things I hear from boys in secondary schools is: 'I like teachers who earn my respect and don't just expect it.' This is closely followed by, in some form or another: 'I like teachers who are friendly and fun but also firm and fair' and 'I like teachers who get on well with students but who are strict when necessary.' Part of earning boys' respect is building relationships with them, taking the time to understand them better, and working hard and having fun together. One struggling Year 10 boy quoted a teacher he greatly admired as saying, 'I'm going to make sure you can do this!' Another boy said, 'It's hard to work harder. First day back I think, I can do this! And then it just kind of slips away. I need someone to talk to, and to keep me on the right track. I need someone who has high expectations of me.' As one Year 11 boy a long time ago told me, 'Teachers need to see people for what they are and make them more.'

From these comments, it's clear that while building positive relationships is essential, this should be balanced with setting high expectations and clear rules, and knowing how to enforce them firmly but fairly. For example, it's important to avoid being 'rude', publicly shaming boys and embarrassing them in front of peers.

> **What I'd like to see**
>
> 'A motivated teacher, who doesn't keep having a go at you, sits down next to you and helps you, and isn't just judgemental, can have a laugh with you and then get back to work.'
>
> 'I like teachers who work with you and not against you, who will help you get things right and talk to you privately if you've made a mistake and not embarrass you in front of your friends.'

Above all, boys need to know who's in charge, what the rules are and whether they are being applied consistently. Consistency is something that looms large in the vocabulary of boys, being the most significant element of many areas of education, for example, rewards and sanctions, as we shall see on page 59. A key element of being consistent is not holding grudges and making sure you don't have fixed expectations of a pupil before you've even met them. In terms of those boys who feel as though they want to turn themselves around, they really rate a teacher who 'gives you the chance to redeem yourself' and even 'gives you a fresh start every lesson'.

The meaning of respect and consistency is perhaps best summed up a group of Years 9, 10 and 11 boys in a Midlands secondary school who were in broad agreement on all of the following. They liked teachers who:

- are not mardy
- understand you
- are firm
- don't think they're better than you
- motivate you
- are never bossy or rude
- are fun
- don't throw a fit if you don't have a pencil

- allow you to open windows
- set expectations after they've met you, not before
- are understanding and know where you're coming from.

Being real

A number of years ago now there was a TV programme about education that was virtually unique in its genre in so far as it wasn't merely a series of stunts or stories intended to titillate and amuse. Rather, it presented a useful opportunity to make salient points and promote debate in schools and the wider community at large. The programme was called *Educating Yorkshire*, and I would dare to say, and in fact virtually every day when I'm working with teachers I do say, that this is the best programme on education that I can remember. The response very clearly indicates that I'm not alone in thinking this. Why was it so powerful? Because it showed us just how important it is that as teachers we bring our personalities to school, that we are real people and are here for all youngsters. As teachers, we know that there are many children in our care for whom nobody's eyes light up when they go home. We know full well that if a child is loved then they come to school to learn. If they're not loved they come to school to be loved and it is so important that we are here and we are real people for them. The other major theme of the series was just how important it is that we never give up on those individuals pupils. If you could watch that final programme, with the boy who could previously barely speak, without shedding a tear, you're a stronger person than I am, that's all I can say. (At the time of writing, the programme is still available through the Channel 4 website, if you haven't yet seen it.)

> **What I'd like to see**
>
> 'I like teachers when they don't pretend they are perfect and show us what kind of person they are.'
> '[I like teachers who] don't pretend to be like royalty and patronise you.'
> Boys rate teachers who 'get to know you' and 'bond with you', 'have a sense of humour and are not mardy'.

Does the gender of the teacher matter?

Over the years, parents of primary-aged children have been crying out for male teachers to 'Do the discipline!' and 'Take the football!' Wrong! Those aren't even the kind of male teachers that boys love. They like male teachers who are friendly and fun but also firm and fair. In the entrance of a primary school I was visiting a few years ago, they had poems that the children had been asked to write about their teachers (try it!). I stole snippets from four:

> 'Mr Copnall is a drink of fizzy coke.'
> 'Mr Nash is a chocolate bar, nice and creamy.'
> 'Mr Farrington is a glass of red wine that gets better with age.'
> 'Mr Malacaso is the month of June when the sun comes out.'

(I hope all my male teaching colleagues relate to at least one of these descriptors, and hopefully it's not just the wine one!) One Year 7 boy told me that what he particularly liked was 'When an English teacher is so expressive you feel like you're really in the story.' All this tells us that boys are more concerned with how enthusiastic a teacher is and how much he or she, as one boy once told me, 'wants to teach you and wants you to succeed' than they are about the gender of the teacher. Above all, it is clear to us as teachers and equally as clear to boys that it is all about the quality of relationships. As a Year 10 boy once declared, 'If a teacher you have a decent relationship with says, "I was really disappointed in you this lesson" and you have that bond with them, then you'll try hard next time to turn it around.' Another added, 'It's good when a teacher understands about your home life and understands that you might be having a bad day.'

In fact, whenever the issue has arisen, and it's almost always me that brings it up (!), the gender of the teacher is generally seen as largely irrelevant, although I do on a rare occasion hear a preference expressed for male teachers, along the lines of, as one boy once put it, 'I like male teachers because they "get you" better.' More commonly, boys tell me all the time that they really value a teacher, male or female, who 'urges you on', 'encourages you' and 'builds up your confidence'. Very common are comments such as: 'It doesn't matter about the age or gender of a teacher, it's about attitude.' However, one boy reflected the view of many when he made reference to a perceived inconsistency in terms of some teachers' treatment of boys as opposed to their treatment of girls when he said that 'some male teachers can be "scary and mean" towards boys but "laid back and nice" towards girls'.

PE teachers

While most boys don't consider the gender of a teacher to be important, it goes without saying that male teachers do have the opportunity to be positive role models for boys. Male PE teachers, in particular, can have a significant influence here. One Year 8 boy once suggested that 'all teachers should be PE teachers because they're more laid back so you can have a laugh, and because they all love their jobs they never seem to get bored like others do (and they're more understanding if you forget your kit!)'. Male PE teachers in secondary schools can be *the* most important role models a boy is going to get, not least if that boy has no male role model at home and, as is the case in many areas of the country, doesn't see a male teacher until he hits secondary school. If his first encounter with a man in a position of responsibility is that PE teacher from *Kes*, it's no wonder we get those locked horns. (I'm happy to say the PE teacher from *Kes* is extremely rare to find!)

As they potentially play such a huge role in a boy's life, I always suggest that male PE teachers should be in charge of zero tolerance on name calling, whether it's sexist, racist, homophobic, or 'nerd', 'geek', 'wimp', and whether it's on the playing field, in the minibus or in the changing room. They should be the ones who stand up in assembly and talk about what it's like to bring up a young family; they should be actively involved as mentors; they should take a leading role in programmes that are targeted at boys and reading; their pictures should be seen around school engaging in reading, and so on. In one school that I visited, all the PE department had been asked to dress up and act out poems from the anthology. Unforgettable!

So, what makes a good teacher?

Below is a fairly comprehensive list of qualifications drawn from a wide range of discussions with boys of secondary age across the UK. You can count yourself a good teacher in the opinion of many boys if, as they say in their own words, you:

- ✓ are a nice person to work with
- ✓ treat us like young adults
- ✓ don't patronise us
- ✓ make work interesting
- ✓ explain stuff
- ✓ are up to date with marking
- ✓ are someone we can talk to
- ✓ talk to us like we're proper people
- ✓ talk with us and not just at us
- ✓ explain where we've gone wrong and how we can put it right
- ✓ give us the opportunity to make amends
- ✓ wander around the classroom, and don't just sit at your desk
- ✓ remind us of the good things we've done
- ✓ treat everybody fairly and don't have favourites
- ✓ are nice and not disrespectful

- ✓ listen to our opinions
- ✓ explain things properly so we understand
- ✓ have a good relationship with your class
- ✓ allow us to get to know your personality
- ✓ plan lessons (!)
- ✓ don't make us constantly write
- ✓ don't repeat work
- ✓ interact with us
- ✓ don't shout
- ✓ make a good role model
- ✓ can build up our confidence
- ✓ make lessons interesting
- ✓ can see our side of things
- ✓ tell stories about yourself to show you're human too
- ✓ can put yourself in our shoes
- ✓ always ask if we understand and keep checking our understanding
- ✓ make sure we get the work done but can still join in with the chat
- ✓ understand our needs
- ✓ can be strict when necessary
- ✓ make me look forward to your lesson
- ✓ can have a laugh with us and then get back to work
- ✓ show that for you it's not just a job and that you really want to help us
- ✓ don't bear grudges
- ✓ give challenging but not impossible work
- ✓ aren't always acting like you're perfect
- ✓ give us a chance to redeem ourselves
- ✓ can bend the rules a bit
- ✓ adapt to the way we talk and not be too posh because it makes us feel inferior sometimes
- ✓ come round and have a chat
- ✓ greet us personally at the door
- ✓ create a positive atmosphere in the class
- ✓ engage with the class
- ✓ are not constantly in a bad mood

- ✓ are firm, fair and forgiving
- ✓ can control classes
- ✓ constantly support us
- ✓ are friendly and kind
- ✓ don't talk down to us
- ✓ build bonds with a more relaxed way of learning
- ✓ chat with us as we come in.

But perhaps the final word on what makes a good teacher possibly belongs to a young man called Joe who said to me, 'Being a teacher doesn't make you a powerful person; being a nice person does.'

Think

How did you do? I imagine you may have recognised yourself in many of these points. Where is there room for improvement? Make a list and work on it!

Act

How about asking a group of boys in your school about what makes a good teacher? Work through the comments with a colleague and compare them with what *you* think makes a good teacher. What does this exercise tell you both? Is there some common ground to work on? Are there things you can learn between you from the comments of these boys?

Practical exercise

What aspects of your personality, your attitude and your demeanour come across on a regular basis? Put yourself on report today! Create your own report card using the example on the following page as a starting point and record what you notice. Or if you're feeling brave, get the class to create a report card for you and fill it out at the end of the lesson.

Teacher report card

Marks out of five for:

1. Being wide awake and raring to go	1 2 3 4 5
2. Cheerily greeting classes at the doorway	1 2 3 4 5
3. Dealing with any situations with one or two students from the previous lesson as the new class arrives	1 2 3 4 5
4. Keeping an eye out for the boy I crossed swords with yesterday and making a point of smiling at him or praising him	1 2 3 4 5
5. Telling at least one class today that they were my favourite class and saying I was really looking forward to our next lesson	1 2 3 4 5
6. Dispensing the school's (or department's) quota of praise postcards, positive text messages or positive phone calls home	1 2 3 4 5
7. Overall performance in Lesson 1	1 2 3 4 5
8. Overall performance in Lesson 2	1 2 3 4 5
9. Overall performance in Lesson 3	1 2 3 4 5
10. Overall performance in Lesson 4	1 2 3 4 5
11. Overall performance in Lesson 5	1 2 3 4 5

Chapter 7
Getting rewards

> **Overview**
>
> - What kinds of reward work best?
>   - The phone call home
>   - Praise postcards
>   - Quiet approval
>   - Short-term is best
>   - Passing on positive feedback
> - How best to give out rewards
>   - Inconsistency is the issue
>   - Know your class
> - Pupil voice on rewards

Boys do tend to need more praise and encouragement than girls do, and we know why: it's because many get so much attention for all the wrong reasons and we have to compensate for that (see Chapter 3, page 21).

What kinds of reward work best?

Within one local authority, I conducted an online attitudinal questionnaire with all primary and secondary schools. Amongst the topics covered was how boys prefer to be rewarded in school. The most popular way, bar none, was the phone call home. So long as it was a positive phone call obviously!

> **What I'd like to see**
>
> 'My mum got a phone call home once to say I'd been doing well. That was brilliant!'

Phone calls home

Home–school communication, I believe it is fair to say, is usually far more regular in primary schools than it is in secondary schools. Not least as there is the potential for daily contact at drop-off and pick-up! It is of course far more straightforward to develop and maintain a dialogue over a year with a single class teacher than it is with upwards of a dozen subject teachers, heads of year, form tutors, senior managers and heads of department. The most common forms of communication tend to be letters or emails about events or trips, examination timetables and results; bewildering details of Ofsted visits are often just published on the school's website. Set against this background, any form of direct personal contact between a teacher and home carries an enormous amount of weight. A positive phone call home tends to be rare in schools, but massively appreciated by so many of the boys I speak to.

So, what is it about the phone call home that boys appreciate and how can we maximise the positive impact? Well, you might do well to ask boys in your own school that very question. From what I've heard, there is something about this highly personalised approach that they love. It's the fact that you have taken the time and the trouble to show them that extra little bit of interest, to show them that you care. A comment I frequently hear is: 'Your mum gets a lot of phone calls home if you're not doing well!'

Act

Ask yourself whether your school has a department, pastoral team or senior management team rota system for positive phone calls home. If not, is that something you could do? Perhaps you could run a trial.

Praise postcards

Praise postcards have been around a long time. Those issued by secondary schools tend to be subject specific and their distribution tends to be fairly ad hoc. They can often be used disproportionately across departments and inconsistently across year groups. Praise postcards can be a bit of a minefield too. If school is using them then there needs to be a steady flow. There's only one thing worse than getting no praise postcards and that's only getting one in five years: just the one praise postcard stuck on the fridge from Year 7, serving as a constant reminder that he did something good, once… *and* it was a long time ago. The impact of a praise postcard can be maximised if it arrives on a Saturday morning so that the whole family can get to celebrate it together and it doesn't get lost during the everyday hustle and bustle. I find that school-designed and school-produced praise postcards with blank space on the back work best because they can be more personal.

> **What I'd like to see**
>
> 'I don't care what they think about me at school but I care what my mum says about me. When I get a praise postcard from school, my mum takes a picture of me holding it and she sticks it on the fridge and I get five pounds.' Year 10 boy

---

Act

Run an art design challenge to produce praise postcards. One school did just that and the new pack of postcards would be opened in assembly to the surprise of everyone. The pupil who'd designed it then received the first card, which they could give to anyone (teachers included), and then everyone, staff and pupils, was given one to give to someone of their choosing. The rest were used by staff until the next batch arrived.

Quiet approval

What do you think is the least popular way to be rewarded among boys in secondary schools? 'In assembly, in front of everybody else.' Nothing new there then! And we know why, don't we? It's the peer police, that group of boys, usually in Year 10, who are telling our boys whether it's OK to care, to share, to feel, to work, to read, to write, to dance, to sing, to do anything. Boys telling other boys what kind of boys they should be. Throughout my career, I noted on so many occasions that Year 8 boy striding out to the front in assembly for an award for sport, acknowledging his mates, firm handshake with the head – no problem. Same boy a few weeks later, 'and here's your reward for contributions to Year 8 poetry' – he'd rather the ground opened up before he reached the stage.

Of course, we always need to ensure that everyone is appreciated for the effort they put into their work. For some, the all-singing, all-dancing presentations at presentation evenings work a treat, but lots of boys appreciate a quiet word in class.

One teacher had a lovely phrase for small gestures of appreciation, such as a quiet word in class out of the earshot of their peers, or even via a chocolate coin sneaked surreptitiously under their exercise book: 'It's something that they can go with and glow with.' This avoids what many boys describe as 'embarrassing' or 'humiliating' praise in front of their mates.

> **What I'd like to see**
>
> 'More praise in lessons from the teacher – not being kept back or anything but rather in passing during the lesson… a quiet "well done", that's good.'
> Year 10 boy

Short-term rewards

The nature of rewards is clearly significant as far as boys are concerned. I've encountered various schemes that are akin to something we used to get in my day with our shopping… Green Shield Stamps! Each stamp was worth something like 0.001 of a penny. We would collect them and eventually we would exchange a book full of them for a gift. Asking one boy what was wrong with that system, he replied, 'Welllll… you have to turn up every day for five years, always on time, always in uniform, never forgetting your homework, never get into trouble or in detention for five years, and you get a… pencil case.' Short-term targets, short-term goals and short-term rewards are vital for boys.

Passing on positive feedback

'They all talk about you in the staff room.' Boys will passionately tell you about this particular form of injustice. How much truth is there here? Complaining about our troublesome pupils is something we do in the staff room, even though we know full well we shouldn't. (Unless of course we're seeking advice from Superteacher. You know the one: 'He works perfectly OK for me.')

Act

Turn this one around and put up a 'good news noticeboard' in the staff room, featuring pictures of the boys you are mentoring or working with on a boys' project. This idea also works well with the 'presentees': the students who just turn up, do their stuff, never get into trouble and never make it onto the radar for any positive reason.

Then invite any adult in the building to put a sticky note next to each boy's face any time they see him doing something positive, helpful or kind, or any time he has produced good work or shown a positive attitude. They should never write anything negative. Then hand over the sticky notes to the boys whenever and however you choose. From the very first moment a boy gets a piece of

> good news from the noticeboard, suddenly everybody becomes desperate for good news. In my experience, it has changed countless boys' attitudes towards themselves and the attitudes of teachers towards those boys.

The above was a technique we used very successfully as part of the National Education Breakthrough Programme of which I was chair for its five years of existence (which is described in Chapter 26). From time to time, the pupils' head of year and form teacher would pass on these comments to the pupil. In the context of the Breakthrough Programme, it changed a lot of boys' attitudes towards themselves, a lot of teachers' attitudes towards those boys, and very usefully, the attitudes of teachers who had never taught those boys, but just heard about them in the staff room.

How best to give out rewards

Here, consistency is key, as is knowing the boys in your class.

Consistency

With regard to rewards generally, inconsistency is a common criticism. As one boy explained, representing the views of many: 'Some teachers give rewards and some teachers don't – when we get to Years 10 and 11, they think that we're not interested in rewards anymore but yes we are!' Another boy said, 'I get a real sinking feeling sometimes when a teacher forgets to give you the reward they promised. It's like they don't really care about you somehow.' 'Yeah,' added another, 'and look at that chart on the wall, look at all them special needs kids, they get an award for just turning up on time and having a pencil. What's the point in *me* working hard?' This is a very difficult thing for me to write, but it is a common perception that students have.

> **Think**
>
> 'People who mess about get rewards for being good once. Consistent students are not rewarded.' Year 11 boy
>
> A very significant point is the plight of the 'presentees' – those who turn up day after day and just get on with what is expected of them. How does this pan out for you at your school? What could you do to improve it?

We know this does happen and boys can become quite irate when discussing this issue. This needs addressing if everyone is to buy into your rewards policy. What are you doing (be honest) and what could you do to improve the situation?

Act

How about agreeing as a department or whole school that you will be constantly reminding classes as and when it is necessary (and certainly no less frequently than at the beginning of each half term) that the reward system is there to show how much school or individual teachers appreciate their efforts. You could back this up with an A4 poster proclaiming:

We give rewards for:
- a great effort with a piece of work
- a significant improvement in behaviour or attitude
- working consistently well over a period of time
and so on.

One boy said to me quite simply, 'I've never been praised. Not once.' On a similar theme, one newly appointed head of Year 8, at the end of the first term, told me, 'I haven't been sent a "good boy" yet.' We need to get it together to get them together!

Act

In conversation with countless numbers of boys, the view of one young man about rewards and punishments was extremely common. He said, 'In our school, it's easier to get a demerit than it is to get a merit.' Does that apply to your school? Do certain groups of boys feel this is the case? Have you asked them recently? Have the discussion, as senior managers with a cross sample of boys.

Know your class

Knowing your class well will determine just how you dispense praise and appreciation, varying from a quiet word, a note left discreetly in their pupil planner, very specific praise for their role in group work, or that phone call or text message home. You will know that the more public praise may not suit everyone, for example, the ticks amassing on the board in the context of competition or challenge, public praise in the classroom or assembly, or sharing work by displaying it.

Listening to the boys in your school

My most er… rewarding experiences of reward schemes have been where the youngsters themselves have been asked to collate opinions from their peers about the way they like their achievements celebrated and what form their rewards should take. Subsequently they have devised the school's reward system and presented it to the staff, very often in a formal staff meeting. Boys often become quite animated when discussing appropriate rewards, from free prom tickets and sports gear to being allowed to listen to music in headphones, early dinner passes and, way down at the bottom of the list… stationery (the most common physical reward but hardly designed to fire up a boy's enthusiasm for work!).

In one school, heads of year selected two 'students of the week': one boy and one girl who had produced some excellent work or exhibited kindness or helpfulness. Those who have achieved above and beyond receive the head's handshake, which, in turn, was equivalent to five house points. For all of the above, part of their reward was breakfast in the head's office with the head or pastoral head (the head in this school said it was the highlight of his week, as the pupils were all keen to talk about what they thought about school matters). One boy at the school talked about other positive elements of the school's reward policy: 'We get rewards that are educational trips. Educational trips give you the chance to increase your learning more by actually being there and processing it.'

However, it's not enough to just look at the kind of rewards we use in school, more importantly, it's about creating a positive achievement culture within the school, so that everyone can take pride in achieving the best that they can, and being the best that they can be, but also confident that they can celebrate their achievements without fear of reprisals from their peers. We also need to ask the experts about this too. One such expert, Darren, aged 12, told me, 'We don't need to be bribed; we need to be appreciated.' Another declared, 'Detentions and that kind of thing just don't work. It's down to yourself; you have to decide you want to do better.' Others have expressed the view that 'We shouldn't be bribing people to attend school' and 'Allowing Year 11s to jump the dinner queue if they've been good isn't fair.'

It's also important to take into account the age of the pupils. I've heard some older pupils say, 'Rewards work for Year 7s', so there is undoubtedly a case for age-related rewards, rather than the same rewards throughout, but as always I would say – ask the experts!

Practical exercise

Here is a template for a pupil voice exercise in putting together a reward system (adapted from *Breaking Through Barriers to Boys' Achievement*). This can be a very straightforward but significantly useful first activity to conduct with a team of pupils responsible for bringing about change (such as the 'Changemakers' in Chapter 24). A questionnaire containing the questions below could be administered by a form tutor in tutor time or by a team of pupils working with groups of pupils, and their findings delivered by them in a staff meeting and subsequently in assembly. Add your own questions based on what *you* want to find out from your pupils. A sample of one form's responses could be taken from each year group in order to help them ascertain the levels of enthusiasm for each year group. This would also help them to ascertain preferences by age group, and so on. Use the results of this survey, whether it be from just a class (or two) or the whole school, to form the basis of the school's new reward system.

Pupil survey: School reward system

- Do you like it when a teacher comments positively about your work in front of the whole class?
- Do you prefer just a quiet word as the teacher passes by you in class?
- Do you like it when your work is displayed?
- Would it be best if the teacher mentioned it to you first?
- Are you happy reading your work out in front of the class?
- Would you prefer it if your teacher did it?
- Do you like to have your name read out in assembly for good work?
- Are you happy to receive an award in assembly?
- Do you like praise postcards?
- What about letters home (containing good news)?
- What kind of rewards would you appreciate?

Chapter 8
Punishments

> **Overview**
> - Inclusion: ban the booths
> - Detentions don't work
> - Writing as punishment
> - Alternative sanctions: can't we just talk about it?
> - Restorative justice

One troubled Year 10 boy told me in front of his friends, in discussion: 'When I've been suspended, it means I'm not there and so nobody has to deal with it. Then you go back and you're behind with everything and you just wait for it all to start all over again. It's here we go again... Being kicked out should be the very last thing that happens.' Another concurred, 'Yeah, I think getting kicked out of the classroom should be the very last thing to happen, but it happens to me all the time. Certain teachers don't go through the system. I just get sent straight out. It's because of my reputation. I got excluded last year because there was a "probability" I'd done something wrong. A probability!' I asked if his parents were worried about him. 'Yeah, thing is I don't care about the punishments in school but I do care what my parents think.' I asked how it feels when he gets praise or a reward in school. He told me, 'It feels good to make my mum feel proud – that's a good thing. The thing is though, in school they're really quick to tell you when you're doing something wrong but really slow to let you know when you're doing the opposite.'

On a 'learning walk', a senior member of staff and I were walking along a corridor when the senior member of staff halted a boy to congratulate him on his recent success in a drama production: a delight to hear a mature young man being complimented and accepting the praise gracefully. Upon setting off in opposite directions, the teacher's final comment was, 'Oh, and tuck your shirt in, will you? You look a mess.'

Surely there has to be a better way?

'Inclusion' doesn't work

A regular Year 10 visitor to 'inclusion' – in other words, isolation – told me, 'I hate it. You're just sitting there on your own. Trapped with your own thoughts. Literally you're in a box.' Another said, 'Today I got really excited because I heard there was going to be a fire drill so I'd get to stand outside for ten minutes.' And there's more: 'Sitting in that box isn't gonna sort it out. I'd rather be expelled. I just go from inclusion, every day I'm in there, with more anger.'

In January 2020, in the north of England, there was a campaign 'to lose the booths' and there was even a conference of the same name. Anne Longfield, Children's Commissioner for England reported that some pupils told her they had been put in isolation repeatedly for days or weeks at a time and described the experience as 'distressing and degrading', while others said they had slept because there was nothing to do. The children's commissioner is, at the time of writing, conducting research to find out how widespread the use of isolation booths is and what kind of children are affected, in response to mounting disquiet among parents and mental health campaigners about the practice.

> **Think**
>
> Do you run a similar system in your school? Isn't it time to change?

One boy who, by his own admission, was spending quite a lot of time in corridors or in 'inclusion' told me: 'What I did yesterday in geography was I got sent out. This morning I went and apologised to him and we had a serious chat and he said he'd try and get me out of inclusion and back into lesson.' (The punishment for disciplinary issues lasted from a day to a full week.) 'It felt like I'd had to do something bad to get his attention. But when I did, he helped me. Inclusion's bad. I'd just rather sit down with the teacher and sort it out.'

" What I'd like to see

'If a teacher behaves more like a person than a teacher then you're going to respond more positively. If they have a quiet word with you at the end of a lesson and say something like, "I was very disappointed in your behaviour today," you're probably going to try harder next lesson. If they say nothing to you and just give you loads of penalty points or send you to inclusion, it just makes you resentful. It doesn't make you want to change.' "

Detentions don't work

'Detentions don't work, do they?' one Year 9 boy announced to me, echoing the voice of hundreds – teachers and boys alike, 'They can put you right off a subject an' all.' His friend added, 'They definitely don't work, and it's mostly boys and it's always the same boys. There were three classrooms full last week!' Another boy said, 'You're just sat in a room with all the naughtiest kids in school and they think you're like them.'

Throughout my 27 years of teaching, particularly as a head of department, I have been forced to be in detention for hour after hour after hour, usually with a group that was largely made up of boys, and often the same boys week after week after week after week. Some boys would turn up for detention even when they weren't in detention – they just assumed they were in detention – and sometimes they came along to the detention because their friends were in detention and they wanted to walk home with them after detention.

> **Act**
>
> Hold a pupil voice session around sanctions. When you ask the boys (they also know detentions don't work), you'll find their ideas for dispensing punishment range from the quite sensible – detentions at lunchtime, losing social time rather than after school, being made to do something boring, missing out on their favourite lesson – to the more draconian, starting at caning and stopping just short of hanging, drawing and quartering.

Just a few issues a group of Year 10 boys raised with me with regards to detention include:

- 'If I get a detention, I'm not allowed my phone for a week! That means like no social life. How would teachers feel without their phone for a week? There should be more leeway with punishments.'
- 'Some lads brag about how many detentions they're in.'
- 'Detentions and that kind of thing just don't work. It's down to yourself; you have to decide you want to do better.'

As for widely used penalty points, which then add up to detentions over time, a group of boys in another school offered, with an air of bemusement:

- 'You get penalty points for forgetting a pencil, wearing the wrong trousers, an unfastened top button, wearing the wrong socks.'

- 'Yeah, imagine this though: it's totally demoralising when you get a detention for rolling your sleeves up... it's a lot easier to get put down than it is to get rewards.'
- 'It's five points in a term and it's detention – I got four in one day once at the beginning of term so I've not much chance. Being on four points is really stressful.'

Talking about demoralising, a boy in the same group said to me, 'I did my homework in pencil once and the teacher just sat there and rubbed it out in front of me and made me do it again.' This school recently changed the system and allowed teachers to use reward points to remove penalty points. This had been a reasonable success. However, problems still remained. One Year 9 boy asserted, 'Parents don't really see what you're getting penalty points for – or rewards for that matter. The wording they choose on reports makes it sound more serious.' Others said, to murmurs of agreement around the group:

- 'Five penalty points and you get a letter home. 100 rewards and you get nothing.'
- 'My mum says all she gets from school are detention letters, and the thing is, some teachers give rewards regularly but others don't. If I had a bit more recognition for my work it would keep me a lot more engaged.'
- 'I'll tell you what else as well. When girls all sit at the back, the teacher says nothing, but when we do, the teacher goes straight to penalty points – they're trigger-happy some of them.'
- 'You know what? I've never seen a single girl get a penalty point.'

> **What I'd like to see**
>
> 'The problem is the wording of penalty points can look quite harsh. It can be a box to tick that says something like "Persistently disrupted", but the crime might be less than that. It makes it look really bad and then I get it in the neck from my parents. I'd like the wording to be made simpler.'

Writing as punishment

Still massively common, and detested by boys and many teachers alike, is setting writing as punishment. So, it goes, the boy's done something wrong and he's given a piece of writing as punishment. The next day the boys got the same teacher for a lesson and the teacher says, 'Right boys, we're going to do some writing now.'

'Why? What have I done wrong now?' replies the boy.

'What do you mean?'

'It's punishment…'

'Noooo, no, that was yesterday.'

It just doesn't compute. It's no wonder this boy wrote as part of his self-evaluation in his final Year 11 report: 'I will continue to work hard and do my very best regardless of how pointless the task is.'

Think

Is writing ever given as punishment at your school? What are your thoughts on this? What do boys think about that?

Act

Ban the use of writing for punishment. Now! But only if you want to improve boys' attitudes towards writing! And only if your boys don't tell you, 'It's brilliant writing something out for no particular reason. I love it.'

One religious studies teacher told me that he decided to give one of his bright Year 11s a two-part written challenge to complete in a detention, and said that when finished to the teacher's satisfaction, he could go. The question was in two parts: 'Can you write a letter to God saying how you feel living at this moment in history and then write the reply?' The boy responded, 'Dear God, what the hell are you doing? It's a real nightmare down here.' The teacher, somewhat dumbfounded but adamant that the boy should lose a fair chunk of his time, not just a matter of seconds, then asked for the reply. 'Dear Nathan, as you know, I am a listening God. I do not interfere.' Detention over, five minutes in.

It's a similar problem with any task a pupil might also be expected to complete in class. When reading is the task they're given in detention, for example, as one Year 8 boy put it quite simply, 'It means I now associate reading as punishment.'

What are the alternatives?

Maybe most useful of all was the idea of a wayward Year 8 in detention: 'I think it would be better if I could just sit down with the teacher and we just talked about what had happened and why, and what I can learn from that.' Another boy said, 'The best thing is when you can talk it through with the teacher when the anger's gone.'

Sanctions at home may be: he's made a mess of his room so he needs to tidy it up. He's not put his clothes in to wash so he needs to do his own washing. He's arrived home later than he promised so he has to make his own tea. In school, sanctions may be: he's messed about in class, or he's forgotten his homework repeatedly, or he's not completed work on time, or he's been rude to the teacher, or he's been sent out of a lesson. The sanction for all of these? Detention. Not even the same day, and more often than not, not even with the teacher involved.

Think

Can we do better than that?

Act

Work on alternative strategies to avoid the need for detentions. For example, as suggested in the Year 8 group discussion with regard to dealing with some behaviours, you could arrange a shorter period of time spent after school with the victim and the perpetrator (as in restorative justice, see below). In that way, we can 'hear him out, and it would make more sense'. Or, how about:

- lunchtime behaviour workshops
- lunchtime mindfulness sessions
- lunchtime yoga or meditation sessions
- lunchtime positive mindset workshops?

Restorative justice

Finding favour in schools in recent years, as a means of talking disciplinary issues through to sort them out, is restorative justice. Restorative justice is a means by which problems and conflicts between two parties can be addressed and hopefully resolved. It draws two people together in conversation, during which the perpetrator explains what they did and why, and then the victim describes how they felt about the experience and finally what the perpetrator can do to make amends. Sometimes one of them resists, in which case a mediator can be employed. (That's where you come in!) Restorative justice includes questions to both the harmer and the harmed.

Practical exercise

Try planning a restorative justice session using the following sets of questions.

Questions to the harmer:

- What happened?
- What were you thinking about at the time?
- What have your thoughts been since?
- How do you feel about what's happened?
- Who has been affected by what you did?
- What do you think should be done to make things right?

Questions to the harmed:

- What happened?
- What were your thoughts at the time?
- What have your thoughts been since?
- How do you feel about what's happened?
- How has this affected you and others?
- What has been the hardest thing for you?
- What do you think needs to happen to make things right?

Chapter 9
Peer pressure

'Be nice to nerds. Chances are you'll end up working for one.'

Charles J. Sykes

> **Overview**
>
> - The peer police cadets: Year 6 boys who drag other boys off cliffs
>   - The Transformers: giving peer police cadets responsibility
> - The peer police: peer pressure in secondary schools and the impact in Year 8
>   - The Anti-Bullying Massif
>   - Holding up work in class
>   - Hassle and how to deal with it

Who was it who said, 'Never doubt that a small group of people can change the world'? It's always been the case. What about the small groups of boys that exist in many, many schools in Year 10, who are telling other boys whether it's OK to care, to share, to feel, to work, to dance, to sing, to write, to read, virtually anything? A group of boys who are telling our boys exactly what kind of boy they should be. I call them the 'peer police'. A small group of boys who can change the world on a daily basis for so many. Of all the barriers to boys' achievement, peer pressure can be one of the most significant, and as we've seen, it begins in the nursery: 'You can't wear that. You're a boy and that's pink! What are you playing at?' It develops into a fairly well-known phenomenon by the time they reach Year 6.

The peer police cadets

My experience of working with teachers from hundreds and hundreds of primary schools across the length and breadth of the UK is that in virtually every single Year 6 class there is a small group of boys whom I call the 'peer police cadets': a group of boys who are trying to drag other boys off cliffs. The only area of disagreement I've encountered from time to time when discussing this issue with hundreds of Year 6 teachers is with the word 'small'.

At the opening conference of a project I was running in Bradford a number of years ago, with 28 primary schools, I asked all the heads if they had a group of boys in Year 6 who were trying to drag other boys off cliffs. All said they had, apart from two who said, 'They're in Year 5 this year but they're coming up.' To all, I recommended that they give their groups of boys a positive focus for their natural leadership abilities. I gave them lots more advice, including giving their group a positive title (remember my Top Lads from Chapter 2?) and making sure as heads that staff would be fulsome in their praise and enthusiasm for the group's efforts. One headteacher approached me at the end and said how she would certainly be trying it: 'I've got this lad, Jack. Jack the lad, yes, I've even called him Jack the lad to his face, but not anymore, not er... not since I've been to your conference. I'm going to ask him if he's got any ideas about how we can raise money for the school that we're twinned with in South America.' So she did. 'I could do a sponsored BMX ride around the playground,' was his immediate response. So, the head, convinced that no harm could come to anyone just riding round and round the playground, immediately said yes. Come the day, his dad arrived with a lorry load of wooden pallets and huge wooden cable rolls. It was a rainy, greasy day, parents were gathering and you're doing a risk assessment as I speak – I know, I can tell! He leaped from rickety pile to rickety pile. The boy's performance was spectacular, and from that moment on, having enjoyed all the attention for such a positive effort on his part, Jack and his little group of acolytes started to drag other boys up mountains as opposed to dragging them off cliffs.

Giving the peer police cadets responsibility

'Come on, you can help us with this. You can help us with that.' A big part of the reason for the success of my project in Bradford was the fact that I recommended that schools called their small band of peer police cadets 'The Transformers'. Oh, they loved that. Sometimes they were asked to help out in Reception with reading. The schools had special stickers made: 'Helped By The Transformers'. Helping out with eco-friendly projects around the school was another winner: 'Sorted By The Transformers'. It worked so well that I thought this can't be a fluke. I tried it again and again and again and again. In one local authority, 24 primary schools adopted the Transformer scheme simultaneously. This time, Transformers from small clusters of schools across the authority would frequently meet together to share ideas and work on projects, from producing birdfeeders to creating sensory gardens, from reading to little ones in the nursery of their own school to teaching the very youngest how to play outdoor games. At the end of the year, the heads from all the schools brought along their Transformers to celebrate their achievements together at their local football club's stadium: a place special to many of them! These were boys who previously had been dragging other boys off cliffs.

The peer police in secondary schools

On a similar basis a project was dubbed the 'Anti-Bullying Massif' in an inner London secondary school, where a group of boys were told, 'We're going to put you in charge of bullying' and they went 'Ooh... great!' 'No, no, no, put you in charge of getting rid of bullying – you don't understand. We're going to send you on a listening skills course and a peer mediation skills course, and you're going to work in the playground with the bullies and the victims. We're going to give you a budget so you can develop a poster campaign and open up a drop-in centre.' They did it so well that they ended up delivering training in other schools to show them how they could do it.

As we have seen, peer pressure starts at a very early age, but when it comes to secondary education, Year 7s are very much tied up with transition and settling in, Year 9 is very much to do with options and, at the time of writing, the beginning of GCSEs for many, and Years 10 and 11 GCSEs. Year 8 can be a bit of a vacuum for boys, a point at which a lot of boys can start to orientate themselves away from education, often because they come under the cosh of the peer police.

Peer pressure at its worst can be a particularly pernicious form of bullying, being that its main purpose is to force our boys into being what kind of boys they should be, according to the boundaries laid down by the peer police. It can be a tough call, for example, turning up on the first day at secondary school with a violin case if you're a boy. I met a teacher a few years ago who said that when she was at school she was a twin (well she still is!) and that every Monday morning when they reached the school gates her brother would ask her, 'Can you take my cello case up to music for me, sis?' And every Monday for five years she did. He ended up playing cello in the Hallé Orchestra in Manchester. Thank goodness he had a sister, but it shouldn't have to be that way. At that point of transition, it is so important that as primary teachers and secondary teachers alike, supported by parents, we help them across that great divide. Apart from anything else, if we're trying to turn out decent young men, the expressive, creative and performing arts can be a huge part of this. As we all know, as secondary teachers, if we can get the peer police on board with a school production, fashion show, revision club, and so on, then suddenly it's all right for all boys to engage.

> **Think**
>
> How aware are you as a school of the impact of negative peer pressure on the achievement of boys? What examples can you think of where this has happened? What can you do to minimise and ultimately eradicate negative peer pressure? The sooner we help boys deal with negative peer pressure, the better.

Holding up work in class

In discussion with a group of high-flying Year 8 boys, I found they hated it when a teacher showed their work to the rest of the class. It was a crushing experience for them. But, as one pointed out, it was also a crushing experience for those whose work was not deemed worthy of praise. Indeed, there was a general expression of dismay at the mere mention of such practices. 'You get a real sinking feeling,' said one. 'I just hate it,' said another. The same boy could understand why the teacher would do such a thing but wondered if they had ever considered that perhaps they were presenting pupils who 'weren't so bright' with an 'impossible task', thus dispiriting them rather than encouraging them. 'They might think, I could never do work as good as that.' Each of the boys in the group cited examples of when their work had been 'held up' in such a way at some time or another, and each one reported that to some degree they 'got some stick for it' from other members of the class, often their own friends. One boy said he was repeatedly teased for it for a week.

In discussion with another small group of high-flying boys in a particularly challenging school, the group expressed no surprise that there were disproportionate levels of achievement at GCSE between girls and boys, declaring, 'Girls just get on with it… They're more… They put the work in. They just seem to care more. Boys don't work as hard because they worry they'll get more stick from their mates if they do.' And 'Girls get more worried about their work… They panic… They're fussy.' 'Boys leave their work to the last minute.' One admitted that even he tended to leave it to the last minute, but, he stressed, it always got done. With regard to what motivates them to work hard, whilst many of their male peers might not be so well motivated, one offered a personal account: 'Well, the thing is with me, I've worked with my dad in his factory, just at weekends and holidays. And it's… well, it's… boring… it's monotonous like… but just feeding machinery… I mean… but there are lads there that'll be doing that for the rest of their lives and well… it's not for me. It makes me think, well, if I knuckle down I won't have to do this kind of thing.' As far as the whole group was concerned it was simply the thing to do: 'If it's there I do it. There's no point in not doing it… 'cos all that happens is if you don't do it you get hassle off people.'

Hassle and how to avoid it

The issue of hassle and how to avoid it was something that the boys in the group returned to several times. It was commonly used as a defence mechanism that the boys had used in other contexts. The avoidance of hassle, for example, served as a reasonable excuse for working, when they were under pressure from their peers not to. One boy told me, 'I desperately wanted to revise but my mates insisted on coming round to collect me to go off round town. I told my mum to tell them I'd been grounded for a week.'

> **Think**
>
> How extensive is your experience with negative peer pressure?

> **Act**
>
> Through discussions with groups of boys, discover the various ways in which peer pressure impacts on their happiness and their schoolwork. How are they managing that situation? Do they need your help? (Yes, they most certainly do!)

'At a parents' evening,' one boy told me, 'my parents were told "he's very bright but he needs to contribute more in class".' The boy's parents had only recently discovered from their boy that showing the teacher that he understood the work, or he had a contribution to make, was out of the question bearing in mind the amount of 'stick' he would get from his mates. A severe case of peer pressure, which school needed to be aware of and deal with.

But then, peer pressure is everywhere. What about the peer police, the lemon suckers and the mood hoovers in the staff room? The physical space they inhabit? The power they hold? The negative impact they have? Peer pressure is something we need to be aware of and fight against all of our lives.

Practical exercise

Bring peer pressure to the (discussion) table with a small group of forthcoming older boys (include a significant proportion of boys who you know, or suspect, have been at the receiving end of negative peer pressure). Together discuss peer pressure. Compile a list of symptoms or tell-tale signs of peer pressure in both the victims and perpetrators. Together produce a set of guidelines for staff and pupils.

Chapter 10
Academic setting

'Treat people as if they were what they ought to be and you can help them to become what they are capable of.'

Goethe [paraphrased]

Overview

- The impact of setting, and what this means for disadvantaged pupils
- Misallocation: setted by behaviour?
- No movement
- Within-class attainment grouping
- Resistance to change

In all of the research cited by the Education Endowment Foundation (EEF; 2018), it is clear that, on average, 'setting or streaming – where pupils with similar levels of current attainment are grouped together for lessons – is unlikely to boost learning for all pupils.' A large correlational study in the UK, comprising 127 schools and 24,742 pupils, found no overall effects on GCSE performance of setting in English, mathematics or science. However, what is crystal clear from all the research is that disadvantaged pupils are likely to do relatively worse when in sets organised by attainment.

The impact of setting

Of all the topics covered in my discussions with boys, setting is often one that many have lots to say something about, whether they're in the bottom, middle or top sets. Boys in the bottom sets say:

- 'Bottom sets make you feel like you're rubbish.'
- 'They're demeaning.'

- 'Sets just give you a label.'
- 'If you're in bottom set, what's the point?'
- 'Bottom sets demotivate you and make you feel bad.'
- 'You feel like people don't care about you.'
- 'You get respected more by teachers if you're in top sets.'
- 'I'd like to be in top sets so I can be with the kind of boys I aspire to be.'

Boys in the top sets say:

- 'They expect too much in top sets. They kind of like assume you know everything and they rush you.'
- 'We are judged by our sets. Expectations are very high for top sets.'

And in the middle sets, the perception of many boys is that schools care more about top sets and that it is sometimes even to the detriment of pupils in middle sets. One boy declared, 'Students in the middle can be forgotten. There's lots of praise for the top students, as you might expect, and lots for bottom-set students for just doing a simple thing.' Another told me, 'When I asked the teacher about why I was in a middle set, he told me not to worry 'cos they teach us the same as the top class, so I thought, why split us up then…?'

> ### What I'd like to see
>
> 'Sets label you too much. You see the label "Foundation" on your mock maths paper – it's not going to motivate you. You're gonna go – why bother? Get rid of the "Foundation" label and they might do better. It's like a mental label – I'm Foundation, I can't do more than this.' Year 11 boy

Personally, I have always thought that you don't put the linguistically most deprived in the linguistically most deprived environment and hope to make a difference.

> **Think**
>
> I have always thought that it is arrogant of me to think that they are learning everything from me. They're learning just as much from each other. What do you think?

In my sessions for parents, I cover the business of setting. It can still touch a nerve many years after a person's experience of it. One father in his 40s came up to me at the end of a parents' session on one occasion and said, 'Please don't ever stop saying what you're saying about setting. I spent 20 years of my life thinking I was rubbish.'

During the context of a full day's work in a secondary school, I asked to go on two 'learning walks,' one looking in on bottom sets and the other on top sets. It was quite stunning. It was the member of the SLT who accompanied me who was the first to utter, 'Those were two completely different experiences. It was like visiting two completely different schools.' If it has that kind of impact on two education professionals on a fleeting visit, what impact can it have on the pupils on a day-to-day, day-in-and-day-out basis?

> **Act**
>
> With a colleague, try the two learning walks described above: the first focusing exclusively on bottom sets and the second on top sets. Observe the differences in teachers' delivery, the geography of the room, levels of engagement, and the difference in interactions with boys and girls (including the frequency and nature of interactions).

Misallocation

In so many discussions, so many boys tell me that they are convinced that they were in lower sets because of their behaviour, which in turn creates its own downward spiral. Within any group of boys, someone will always raise the point that they know categorically that they have been, or their peers have been, put into lower groups because of their behaviour and not because of their ability. There's a word for it: 'misallocation'.

According to the EEF (2018), there is 'evidence from the UK that misallocation to "ability groups" is a particular problem for pupils from disadvantaged backgrounds. These pupils appear to be at greater risk of misallocation to lower attaining groups, and the impact of setting or streaming on pupils in lower attaining groups is negative on average'.

I remember one boy telling me, 'I got moved down in one subject because of my behaviour and my behaviour's worse now in all subjects.' Another said, 'I got told I dominate lessons when I only want to contribute. I talked a lot in Years 7 and 8, so I was dropped down. Then, because the work was so much easier, I didn't feel the need to join in and I didn't need to ask questions.' A third added that he felt it wasn't just his own attitude and behaviour that was affected: 'You end up in lower groups because of your behaviour and the lower you get, the less teachers try.' One teacher, after sitting in on a discussion with a group of Year 10s who had strong feelings about settings, did admit afterwards, 'In our school, from what I've just heard, setting doesn't appear to have a negative impact on boys but it does on staff expectations.'

The impact of setting on behaviour is backed up by academic research, in which criticism of setting is not new. Hargreaves (1982) says, 'Ability labelling strips young people of their sense of being worthy, competent, creative, inventive, critical human beings and encourages them to find other ways of achieving dignity, often through oppositional means.' Often it is not glaringly obvious, as the majority of youngsters attempt to maintain dignity and accept what is happening to them at school without any complaint. But, as Hargreaves points out, 'There is a distinct minority which reacts with overt bitterness and hostility.'

For those who felt that setting was to do with their previous marks or scores, this sentiment was not uncommon: 'There are lots of clever pupils in lower sets because of target grades – they use the grades from primary school and I didn't really care in primary school. I never thought primary school work was important. I thought it only really mattered when you got to secondary school, so I didn't really try my hardest.' In a small group discussion with some Year 9s, one boy suggested that 'there are a lot of clever people in lower sets because of target grades'. His friend agreed and added, 'Yeah, how can the government know that if you get poor SATs you're going to get poor GCSEs? You probably will though because you end up in bottom sets right from Year 7. And then you're not expected to be any good, so you end up feeling less good about yourself... and then eventually you just give up. You think, why bother?'

Moving up (or not)

For many, what really gets to them is the frustration, or to express it more forcefully, the grim reality, that they are in bottom or lower sets and are told they can move up, but they rarely do. Frustrations can build and often lead to low self-esteem, anger and frustration: 'I know I'm in some bottom sets because of my behaviour and I know there's no chance of getting moved up. Nobody I know ever has.' Boy after boy after boy tells me they would like to see more movement in groups. Even just feeling they have a realistic chance of moving up could be an improvement.

What I'd like to see

'They never let a person change. You're put in a bottom set in Year 7 and you're kept that way until Year 11. In bottom sets there's not much chance for movement, which is not good for your behaviour.'

'If you got moved up, it would boost your confidence and it would make you work harder.'

So, what's the answer?

Questioning why setting sometimes didn't seem to make sense, one 14-year-old posed the question, 'In Spanish, it's mixed from foundation to higher. If they can do it, why can't everybody?' On one occasion, a Year 10 boy explained his view thus: 'You can learn more from brainier pupils than teachers sometimes because they explain it at your level.' Another added, 'If your mate's learnt summat you want to too – you don't want to be thick.' So, is there a middle ground?

A much smaller study cited by the EEF (2018) attempted to discover the answer. Their study on 'within-class attainment grouping' found that grouping together pupils with similar current attainment to carry out specific activities within their usual class and with their usual teacher is effective. The EEF research said '[this approach] can lead to average gains of around three additional months' progress per year', although, and here we go again, 'it tends to benefit lower attaining pupils less than their peers'. Steven Higgins in the *Sutton Trust-EEF Teaching and Learning Toolkit* concludes: 'Both types of grouping, be they in sets or within-class attainment grouping, appear to be more beneficial for higher attaining pupils than for lower attaining pupils, and lower attaining pupils tend to be disproportionately from disadvantaged backgrounds.'

The most common feelings expressed about setting, in the mixed groups of boys I have largely held my discussions with, is that in lessons, mixed groups are better. Those who occasionally take the opposing view are small groups of boys from top sets, who value the fact that there are far fewer distractions. But most common are comments such as, 'It's easier in mixed groups because the more able can help the less able.'

There is significant resistance, I have found, within schools to consider changing their systems of pupil grouping. Likewise, the EEF also noted some challenges with their research: 'It was difficult to persuade schools to adopt mixed attainment teaching, which meant recruiting schools to take part was hard.' It is undoubtedly harder to teach in mixed-attainment groups, but we do have a responsibility to deliver quality education to all. And the evidence is clear: so many of our poor, white, working-class boys are not being given the opportunity or the encouragement. Expectations of their future levels of attainment are low, and their own aspirations are often rock bottom. So much is to do with teacher expectations. One teacher told me the other day that in their school they were: 'preparing boys for Strangeways [a Manchester prison] or at best to be white van drivers. We really must up the game.' Re-evaluating academic setting is a good place to start.

Practical exercise

Carry out yourself as an individual, department or SLT a small piece of research into pupils' views on setting. You could ask small, mixed-gender groups or groups of boys with a range of levels of achievement and motivation:

- why they felt they were in certain groups
- about the possibility or likelihood of changing groups
- how they felt the groups they were in might affect their:
  - work rate
  - levels of achievement
  - self-confidence
  - happiness
  - sense of wellbeing
  - aspirations.

Chapter 11
Seating plans

> **Overview**
> - 'Let me sit with my friends'
> - Do your seating plans work?
> - 'I hate boy–girl seating'
> - Rows, horseshoe or groups: flexibility is the key
> - Leave space to circulate

> **Think**
>
> Do you think your seating plans work? Discuss with your class. Discuss with a colleague or your department. What's the consensus?

So long as they appreciate that if they abuse it, they lose it, flexibility with seating plans has to be key. Sometimes boys are working with their friends and sometimes with pupils they've rarely worked with. Allowing them to sit wherever they like with whomever they like for, say, the first two weeks of the year, before presenting them with a seating plan, is fairly common and is a popular idea with lots of boys. It's worth a try, providing the teacher has made it abundantly clear that if it's not working, they will probably be moved for their own benefit.

Sitting with your mates

Boys have a lot to say on this topic. 'Seating plans don't work,' boys tell me over and over again. 'Segregating you from your friends makes the lesson worse,' they say, and is detrimental to their work: 'I hate seating plans. You can get sat next to an annoying person and your work will suffer.' Many say they find they work better with friends:

- 'I definitely work better if I'm sat with my mate.'
- 'If I'm sat next to a mate, I'll try my best to behave because I don't want to be moved back.'
- 'If I get stuck with reading something difficult, I just give Mahdi a nudge and quietly ask him for help. If I get stuck and I'm sat next to someone I don't get on with, I stay stuck.'
- 'I think it's because teachers don't trust us. If I'm sat there next to my mate, we'll learn stuff together. I can help him and he can help me, between us we can put it in words we both understand.'

And besides, separating friends doesn't necessarily lower disruption. Thinking back to mistakes I used to make, I'd say, 'Right you three!' (They'd not even passed through the door yet.) 'We'll not have you sitting together. We'll have you here, you there and you there.' Then what happened? They'd spend most of the lesson trying to communicate with each other, creating three areas of unrest instead of one. As one boy put it, 'It's nice to sit next to your friend, someone you can trust, can feel relaxed with and besides, most of the noise in the class is people shouting across the room.'

> **What I'd like to see**
>
> 'Let us sit with our friends. At least give us a chance.'
> 'A good lesson is when the teacher lets you sit next to your mates.'
> 'I definitely work better if I'm sat with my friend.'

Boy–girl seating

A common sentiment is: 'I don't like boy-girl-boy-girl seating. It's usually boy-girl-girl-boy-girl-girl-boy. It's never girl-boy-boy-girl-boy-boy-girl!' But of course, this seating arrangement is a common strategy, as alluded to earlier, to raise boys' achievement. In my experience it doesn't raise boys' achievement; rather it raises girls' hackles. And in the top sets they run out of boys, and there are hardly any girls in bottom sets.

Rows, horseshoe or groups?

Of course, never afraid to state the obvious (as you may have already spotted from time to time!), I'd like to point out that different seating arrangements in a classroom suit different activities. Sitting in rows is useful for one-to-one discussions and working individually. On the other hand, sitting as a group whilst you're expecting learners to produce a piece of work individually can mean there are potentially more distractions. We spend a huge amount of time planning what we are going to teach, but how much time do we spend thinking about creating the most effective learning environment? Sitting in rows facing the front harks back to Victorian times when children were the receivers of knowledge from the teacher upfront (that stating the obvious thing's moving into overdrive now, eh?). Have we reverted to that now, with the almighty whiteboard out front? And the 'sage on the stage'? Are we assuming all of the learners in the room work best in that format or are we open to changing seating on a regular basis? Isn't flexibility the key?

Rows can prevent you from seeing everybody, so how about the horseshoe, for all eyes on you and all pupils contributing in discussion? Or two semicircles? Sitting in groups facilitates group work and group discussions, of course, but if they're (sadly) not getting much of those, then should we organise the class in that way all the time? Too hectic, too dangerous, too time-consuming to change tables around speedily? It's amazing how quickly they'll sort the room out for you if it means 'something different today'! When it comes to arranging the seating in your classroom, there isn't a single right way. But it is definitely wrong not to have even thought about it.

Think

When was the last time you changed the seating arrangement in your classroom? Are you willing to regularly change the seating arrangements of your room to provide for all preferred ways of working and all preferred ways of learning?

By the way, really important is to leave space for yourself to circulate around the classroom. It's what so many boys in so many discussions have told me about teachers they really appreciate:

- 'I like when the teacher wanders around when you're working and they have a quiet word.'
- 'Walking round encouraging you, instead of just sitting at the front, is definitely best.'

> **Think**
>
> Try for a week walking around a bit more than you usually do. Notice any difference? Did the class? Maybe ask them what they feel about it?

And one final point on seating plans. This comes up on a regular basis: 'I've seen my name and other people's names highlighted on seating plans for supply teachers.' How do you think that makes the pupil feel and what impact is this likely to have on their behaviour?

Practical exercise

Are you up for a 'sit where you like' day? How about one member of your department volunteering to plan and carry out a 'sit where you like' week? Give it a go!

Chapter 12
How teachers talk to boys and girls

> **Overview**
> - Do we talk to boys and girls differently?
> - 'You know teachers prefer girls, don't you, sir?'
> - 'They think boys are stronger'
> - I don't want to make you feel bad, but show them some love
> - Action research

A friend of mine told me how her daughter, at the end of her first day in nursery, came home and said, 'There are two Neils in nursery, Mummy, and one of them's called Neil Behave! And there's this other one called Gordon Bennett, but I don't know which one he is yet.' Another colleague told me that by the end of her first week her daughter could recite the full names of all the boys but only the first names of the girls ('Gary WILSON, what are you doing? Claire, are you all right?').

Yes, we categorically do talk to boys and girls differently. 27 years of teaching, to the girls, 'That's lovely, dear' and to the boys, 'What are you doing?!'

> **Think**
> Do you think you talk to boys and girls differently? Try this. I want you to close your eyes and imagine it's Friday afternoon (I'm sorry to do this if it's not...). You've got a class in front of you and there's a group of boys at the back of the class, messing about. How are you going to calm them down? 'BOYS!!' Would you believe it, 20 minutes later and there's a group of girls messing about now? How are you going to calm them down? 'Gurrrrls...'

Communication matters

When we communicate, only a small amount of our communication is contained in the words we use. The rest is in our tone of voice, our body language and our demeanour, whether we loom over them or crouch down beside them for a quiet word. So, you might be thinking, 'OK. It's a fair cop, maybe I do, but does it matter?' Actually, yes it does.

Headteacher Peter Downes (2002) did lots of pioneering work into boys and achievement, and one of his main conclusions was that: 'The heart of the issue is the day-to-day relationship between teacher and pupil. The essential theme is that teachers must rethink the language they use when communicating with boys inside and outside the classroom.'

The other reason why how we talk to boys is a hugely significant issue is because whenever I talk to boys about why they're not doing as well as girls, one of the reasons that they come up with as regularly as clockwork in discussions is that teachers prefer girls. The reasons proffered include differential treatment that is meted out in response to misdemeanours. Whenever a boy mentions his first-hand experience, there is suddenly an overwhelming chorus of 'Yeah, and Miss... she never tells the girls off. A boy only has to sneeze. Girls get away with murder.' 'They only seem to notice the bad behaviour of boys. I think it's because our voices are deeper,' one Year 9 boy uttered glumly. And on and on they go until I call a halt. Their main chunk of evidence is almost invariably anecdotal and when I started to hear it over 20 years ago, I thought, that's smart: a deft way of apportioning the blame on teachers. But since I first began this work, I must have heard the same thing thousands of times. It's a very common perception. On one occasion I was speaking to a Year 9 boy who began with the normal refrain:

'Well, you know teachers prefer girls, don't you, sir?'
'What on earth makes you say that?'
'You can tell.'
'Why's that?'
'They don't shout at girls, sir.'
'Why's that, do you think?'
'Because they don't want to make them cry.'
'Really?'
'But they shout at us, sir.'
'Why's that then?'
'Because they think we're stronger.'
'Well, aren't you?' (I was playing the devil's advocate.)
'Well, outside maybe. Outside.'

> **What I'd like to see**
>
> 'They shout at us, sir, because they think we're stronger. I'd like teachers to stop shouting at us.'

Show them some love

The very common perception amongst boys that teachers prefer teaching girls, and that the most obvious manifestation of this is that teachers talk to boys and girls differently, is something that comes up in almost every single discussion. But they're wrong, aren't they? We agreed earlier, do you remember, on page 20? We love teaching boys. We love the fact that they love taking risks. We even love the fact that sometimes they're that little bit more challenging, because that means it can be that little bit more rewarding when they get it right. We love their enthusiasm when we can awaken a real interest in them. We love their openness, their honesty. We love their sense of fun, their sense of humour, and we love the fact that every day's a new day for them.

Enough said? Not quite. Please can you just show that you love them on a more regular basis? Basically, I'm fed up of boys telling me that teachers don't love them and I know full well that you do. My party political broadcast on behalf of the boy party is this: can you please show them that you love them on a more regular basis, because sometimes just that extra little bit of love can go a long, long way?

Now, I don't want to make you feel bad, but I would like you to read this:

'I am the decisive element in the classroom. It is my personal approach that creates the climate. It is my daily mood that makes the weather. As a teacher I possess tremendous power to make a child's life miserable or joyous. I can be a tool of torture or an instrument of inspiration. I can humiliate or humour, hurt or heal. It is my response that decides whether a crisis will be escalated or de-escalated, a child humanized or dehumanized.' (Ginott, 1972)

Act

Copy the above quotation and stick it behind the toilet door in the staff room.

Action research

One school where I made several visits undertook, on my advice, a small piece of action research, whereby they monitored positive and negative comments meted out to boys and girls in the same class, over a 15-minute period. In this case they used in-class support to do the monitoring. This is a snapshot of the results:

Positive comments	Negative comments
'That's right' to boys.	'I need to see your eyes' to boys and girls.
'YES!' to boys and girls.	'You three will get detention if he doesn't do it' to girls.
	'Don't look at them!' to a boy.
	'Dan, grow up!' to a boy.
	'You got that word, Dan?' to a boy.
	'Somebody thinks I'm a god' to a boy.
	'What was the instruction again?' to a boy.
	'Do I speak in a language you don't understand?' to a boy.
	'Do I speak Russian?' to a boy.

I highly recommend this exercise. Sometimes we uncover things we had never begun to consider. In a primary school, for example, where this was tried over the course of a full day, one teacher discovered that they hadn't asked a single boy an open-ended question all day, as they knew instinctively that girls are more reflective. They just asked the boys yes/no questions to make sure they were still alive. The same teacher realised she hadn't asked a single girl a maths question all morning.

Act

Tread more gently, change your tone of voice and inject gentle humour.

Practical exercise

Engage with a piece of action research yourself, based on the way in which we talk to boys and the way we talk to girls. Have one volunteer from each department or faculty undertake this task, using a teaching colleague to do the monitoring.

Chapter 13
Single-sex grouping

> **Overview**
> - My first encounter with an experiment on single-sex grouping
> - Add one laddish teacher: is that a recipe for success?
> - The research: the Homerton Report
> - Mixed results:
>   - 'It worked for me!'
>   - It's all about the teacher

Frequently, teachers ask my opinion of single-sex grouping within a comprehensive school for certain lessons, the most common being science and English lessons. 'The evidence is pretty mixed' is the best I can offer.

My first encounter with an experiment on this was in a large, mixed comprehensive in West Yorkshire around 15 years ago. The subject they had chosen on this occasion was English. My introduction to the class's teacher led me to believe that he was a quietly spoken, middle-aged English teacher, not dissimilar to myself. I was led along to the classroom, and no sooner had I sat down than the quietly spoken teacher transformed before my very eyes into the most laddish of them all. Then the jovial tirade began: 'Right then, Man Mountain, you give out the pencils and you, Face Ache, you give out the paper.' Setting the tone for the whole lesson, it was 'mate this' and 'lad that' and 'kiddo that' and 'laddo this'. I pretty quickly began to feel uncomfortable at the notion that the teacher was going to somehow involve me and that I would be totally embarrassed in front of the class. I'm not big on banter. It was obvious almost immediately that the department had gathered together all 'the lads' into one group and put them in with the most laddish teacher they could find in the hope that there would be a meeting of minds that couldn't happen under any other circumstances. It wasn't for me.

What does the research say?

The Homerton Report (Younger et al., 2005), the country's most extensive piece of research into boys' achievement, focused on single-sex grouping as one of three major strands that might be employed to reduce the gender gap. They closely examined work in three schools. What they found was a very mixed picture. They noted that all-boys classes can be more challenging: 'This was certainly the perception of some teachers in the three schools, and the concern that aggressively macho behaviour was exacerbated simply through a concentration of numbers, with a subsequent worsening of boys' behaviour.' However, in one of the three schools it worked. I continue to come across schools where it has worked and sometimes the boys' responses to the experiment are very positive. One school I have visited had a really positive experience of single-sex grouping. They know because the boys told them throughout the year, in open discussions and ultimately in other ways – for example, by exceeding what was considered to be their likely final grades. The staff were quick to point out, however, that it was virtually impossible to tell if the results of the experiment were down to the quality of the teacher or the make-up of the class. What was useful throughout was that they monitored the effectiveness of the experiment by having a constant dialogue with the boys. At the end of the year they were posed the following question: What would you say has been the biggest benefit to being in an all-boys class with Mr W? The responses were:

- 'Having a great connection with the teacher.'
- 'Being given confidence to ask questions and ask for help.'
- 'Being made more confident to answer questions and not feel embarrassed if I got it wrong.'
- 'Mr W has done the best he could have done for us.'
- 'Mr W provided support such as inviting us to his classroom during lunchtimes for extra work, which helped me to achieve.'
- 'Mr W: he is the best English teacher in the school and he's massively helped me to boost my grades since we started.'
- 'Mr W was great and helped me understand literature a lot better; I think this is solely down to him.'
- 'The biggest benefit is that our confidence has grown. Mr W is supportive with the grades you achieve and he directly works on the weaknesses that the class have.'
- 'Another benefit is that you can talk to Mr W in a one-to-one conversation about the lessons, work and exams, which is a huge benefit for someone like me.'

What is clear from this question is that the boys felt safe and supported in the environment they were in. Having a reassuring and positive role model at the centre of this project had been the defining impact for these Year 11 boys. I would suggest that, as always, the quality of the teacher is the most critical factor and the boys involved were very clear on this point.

> **Think**
>
> Go through all the comments the boys made about Mr W above. Could they apply to any good teacher with a single-sex or mixed group? Which descriptors would you feel roughly describe you and your classroom practice?

The suggestion that girls and boys do better academically if taught separately for some of the time is fraught with difficulty and is often misleading and dangerous. In short, the evidence does not support it. A key survey in this field was conducted by Dr Pamela Robinson and Professor Alan Smithers of the University of Buckingham, who published in 1999 an extensive analysis of the evidence in various countries. Their conclusion was clear: no overwhelming evidence exists that single-sex education is better academically. However, there is significant evidence that children do better socially when educated in mixed groups. In those contexts, boys and girls see things from a range of perspectives and learn to understand the importance of respecting other viewpoints.

Practical exercise

If you are contemplating taking a step in the direction of single-sex grouping, what do you need to think about and why? Consider:

- Is it because you believe girls will benefit from fewer distractions?
- Is it because you believe that *all* boys learn differently from *all* girls?
- Is it because you want to use more 'boy-friendly' resources? Such as?! Do they exist in your subject area?
- Is it a way of improving discipline in a year group by putting all the 'troublesome' boys in the same place?
- Are you thinking you need to put your best teacher in with your most challenging pupils?

Chapter 14
Homework

> **Overview**
> - Setting the right kind of homework
> - Make the purpose clear
> - Homework policies and homework timetables can save a lot of grief in the home
> - Why not do homework at school?
> - Feedback's important

Homework can be a real battlefield for many boys. In fact, homework and writing (see Chapter 16) are two of the most common areas where boys feel frustrated and seek clarity and your support. Boys have told me:

- 'I can't understand why we have to do it.'
- 'We go to school to work. Why should we have to do work at home as well? Home is for relaxing.'
- 'Some teachers get on your back straight away. I forgot my homework a couple of times and for months now I'm the first person the teacher asks for homework *every* single lesson. It really winds me up.'
- 'I did my homework in pencil once and the teacher rubbed it all out in front of me!'

That said, talking to boys in Years 10 and 11, for example, they are quite happy (happy is probably putting it a little bit too strongly!) to do certain kinds of homework: finishing off a piece of work from a lesson or doing some revision. But if it's just a random (they use the word 'random' a lot) sheet of homework that the teacher has given them because (as they know) the headteacher has told all teachers they've got to set homework, and they're never going to see it again, then they're significantly less likely to engage with it.

Making homework relevant

In my experience, asking many boys their opinions about homework will almost always result in, 'We do enough work in school. Why do we have to do work at home?' As we know, if boys don't see a sense and purpose in doing something, they won't blooming well do it, or at least they won't do it to the best of their ability. Therefore, explaining to pupils the purpose of homework is essential when setting it. Teachers shouldn't forget to do this each time they ask pupils to complete a piece of homework.

> **Think**
>
> Do you make it clear to pupils that the purpose of homework is to increase a specific area of knowledge or fluency in a particular area, in order to consolidate the learning?

Research evidence gathered by the EEF (2018) also clearly suggests that relating homework to learning during school hours is important: 'In the most effective examples, homework was an integral part of learning, rather than an add-on.' How teachers feed back on the homework is also crucial: 'To maximise impact, it also appears to be important that pupils are provided with high-quality feedback on their work. Very often, as if to prove this point, the time afforded to setting the homework is very little.' They will complain about instructions being rushed and there being no time for questions if they're unclear, leaving many feeling vague and disgruntled.

> ❝ **What I'd like to see**
>
> 'It makes sense if homework is at the end of a topic as it helps it to sink in.' ❞

Homework and home–school relationships

One boy echoed the responses of many to the specific issues in the home: 'If I'm given extra homework as punishment, my mam's on my back straight away.' So, what could be done to improve communication and clarify expectations with parents and carers around homework?

> **What I'd like to see**
>
> 'Homework creates a lot of trouble at home. It's not my fault if we get lots of homework some nights and sometimes none. Then they don't believe me when I say, "I haven't any tonight." We need a proper planned homework timetable.'

In my experience, it is very common for schools to fail to produce effective homework timetables and to keep them under review so that roughly equal amounts are given each night. This can be fundamental when it comes to eliminating the homework battleground that has such a negative impact on home–school relationships *and* pupil–parent relationships. Indeed, you might argue that clear communication about homework could positively enhance home–school relationships.

> **Act**
>
> Is it fair that sometimes schools don't always check that there is a balance across subjects for homework to ensure that, day by day, pupils get equal amounts of homework? Should we just do a quick health check on the current state of our homework policy? To tighten up on the amounts and the adherence to a fair, balanced homework timetable will have a positive impact on boys, save unrest in the home and reduce our frustrations as teachers.

Texting home to parents about homework

In terms of home–school partnership, many years ago I introduced texting home to parents as part of the reward system in schools across my local authority, starting with the primary schools where, shall we say, Jamal has done a great piece of work in literacy, a message goes down to the office, and the message is texted to the parent: 'Your Jamal has done a great piece of work in literacy.' Brilliant! Dad's on the way to the shops, he's going to buy him a little treat, but most significantly they've got something positive to talk about when Jamal gets home. Latterly, I have recommended its use as part of the reward system of all schools. It needn't stop there. An extended piece of research with 16,000 students in 36 secondary schools across England, the Parent Engagement Project (see EEF, 2016) involved teachers sending roughly 30 texts across the school year to the parents of every pupil involved in GCSE classes. The texts would include prompts for homework, alerts about deadlines, missing homework, dates for upcoming tests, and so on. The research concluded that such an approach boosted the students' maths results by the equivalent of one month in the classroom.

Homework is effectively the bridge between home and school. If schools get communication around homework right, it could potentially enhance parent–child relationships through home learning support.

Some other solutions

Asking for their solutions to the sticky issue of homework will usually result in at least some of the boys suggesting staying on at school or giving them access to a quiet space at lunchtime.

> **What I'd like to see**
>
> 'Why not have an extra period in school to do it?'
> 'It's easier to work at school than it is in our house, so why don't they give us time to do it here?'

Furthermore, boys have often said to me that perhaps a quiz or a test on the key points of the lesson is in itself far more effective in terms of consolidating the learning than a piece of written homework. And that's especially the case for a piece of written work that is produced after a kickabout on the way to the school bus, followed by that long bus journey home and a complete dissection of the previous night's Arsenal debacle, a bar of chocolate and a coke at the corner shop, another kickabout in the back garden and two hours of playing *Call of Duty* eating pizza and chips. The conversation at home might go like this:

'What have you got for homework, Michael?'
'Dunno, can't remember.' (It was two hours ago now.)
'Didn't you write it down?'
'I tried but there wasn't enough time.'

This leads me on to another solution: if we want pupils to complete some homework, we need to make sure we give them plenty of time to note down the homework at the end of the lesson. It's important we don't forget to explain the task and its purpose clearly.

Think

Do we give ourselves enough time to explain the homework carefully, and give them enough time to copy it from the board if necessary? Do we wait until the slowest writer has finished writing it down before the class is dismissed?

Finally, don't forget these key points when setting homework, supported by research collected by the EEF (2018), which is reflected in many of the discussions I have had with boys:

- Do not use homework as a tool for punishment or a penalty for poor performance.
- Set a variety of homework tasks with different levels of challenge.
- Be aware that the quality of homework is more important than the quantity.
- Setting group assignments encourages them to interact with their peers and work together.
- Try using homework to prepare pupils for the work they are going to do the following day.
- Make sure you provide pupils with specific and timely feedback on homework.

In terms of the value of homework, *the* most valuable element is probably the feedback, particularly feedback that is very constructive, that is largely positive and that proves to them that it's not just a random exercise.

Practical exercise

Cast a critical eye over your department or whole-school homework policy in light of the information and advice in this chapter. With your staff or leadership team, work out whether any improvements need to be made with regard to the following:

- What is the purpose of the homework teachers are setting pupils?
- Do teachers make that purpose clear when setting tasks?
- Do you have a fair, balanced homework timetable?
- How do you communicate with parents and carers about the homework being set?
- Do teachers give pupils adequate time to write down homework tasks at the end of the lesson?
- Do teachers provide timely and constructive feedback on homework?
- Is there anything else you could do to improve homework for the boys in your school?

Don't forget to speak with the boys in your school when determining any changes that need to be made.

Chapter 15
Reflection

> **Overview**
> - Tests and quizlets
> - We haven't got time for bloody plenaries!
> - Ofsted and pace
> - Kolb and boys: why reflection matters
> - Questioning in class: name pots, lollipop sticks and a random name generator

In some discussions with boys, I find the irony of the situation comes to the surface on a regular basis for all to see. The conversation might go like this:

'Teachers say we need to take breaks in our revision as a reward every 20 minutes – they told us in assembly it's because it's hard for boys to concentrate for longer. They say that and then we go into our first lesson. It's a double period of English and we have to stay concentrating for an hour and a half.'

'And then we're given an hour's homework.'

'Yeah, and exams are two hours long.'

'At least!'

OK, so we might not be able to change the length of a lesson period or an exam, but what can we do to help? Boys have said to me: 'I like it when we make our own quizlets, learn them and then the next day recall them'; 'Maybe one lesson every five we just do revision instead of revision for homework'; 'I think a small test at the end of a lesson would be much better. It would make sure the lesson had sunk in.' This kind of thing comes up on a regular basis. They're talking about *plenaries*! I know what you're thinking: 'I haven't got time for a bloody plenary and besides, Ofsted insist that we teach at pace.' Actually, Ofsted say 'pace appropriate to the learner', and what is appropriate to these learners is to get them to slow down and reflect on their learning.

> **Act**
>
> With a colleague, jot down all the ways in which you encourage reflection in your lessons. Then share your favourite plenaries or reflection activities with the department or whole school. Share your successes.

Why boys find reflection hard and why this matters

The weakest link in many boys' learning process is their inability to reflect. Remember Kolb's Learning Cycle from teaching training college? It's about how we learn. Read the following out loud in a boring lecturer's voice and it'll come flooding back: 'We have personal experience which we reflect upon and synthesise. We develop an understanding which we can then test out.' Is it working? I'll try it again:

'We have personal experience which we reflect upon and synthesise. We develop an understanding which we can then test out.' However, significant numbers of boys whizz straight through that process of reflection because they just want to get on with the next thing. The worst-case scenario when it comes to reflection, as some of you will remember, was when it came to coursework. The weakest element of boys' work was almost always their inability to reflect. Take PE and drama as just two examples. Their practical work may be really good but what did they have to do at the end of their coursework? Same with PE and design technology? They had to evaluate it: 'It were all right'; 'I did OK'; 'I did this and this happened, I did that and that happened. If only I'd done this, this might have happened.' Like blood out of a stone.

A big part of what we have to do for boys is to get them to slow down and reflect on their learning. For so long we'd ask a question in class and give them seconds to stick up their hands with an answer. There would be two girls over here and two boys over there. We're probably going to choose one of the girls – we want to save time, stay on our agenda and we know they know the answer. If we get the wrong boy it might be: 'Oh… sir, er miss… it's er… I've forgot.' Doing their risk-taking thing, which we admire in some contexts but not here. Meanwhile, there's a group of boys over here, and what are they doing? They're doing mental truancy, that's what they're doing. They don't do questions and answers, do they? They just have a rest whilst everybody else does it. But the problem is, this group of boys is the group that we're most concerned about: the group this book is all about.

This is the group for whom their weakest link is their inability to reflect. But we don't do the forest of hands anymore, do we? We say, 'Right, now with your group, or with your partner, I want you to think about this and I'll come to you at random.' Or, good primary practice, we pick a name out of the name pot, or pick a lollipop stick, or even better at primary or secondary, we use the 'Random Name Generator'. It's free on your smartboard software. You type in everybody's name and you press the button. Lights flash, bells ring. It spins and it stops on somebody's name. There's a cheer and they answer the question. It's a cheap trick, but it works and it's particularly important for our group of boys.

Act

Have a conversation with colleagues about what other techniques you use to help boys to reflect in your lesson. Based on your discussion, try a different way of developing reflection skills.

If you know anybody who still does the forest of hands, and they've got an inspection coming up, you can give them some advice from me. True story. There was an inspector who sat at the back of a classroom next to a boy for a full lesson. Every time the teacher asked a question, every single person in the class put their hands up, and every time the teacher asked a question, the answer was correct. The inspector couldn't believe it. He turned to the boy at the end of the lesson and asked, 'What do you think of that lesson?' and the boy said, 'I'm exhausted!'

'Why's that then?'

'Sticking my hand up all the time.'

'Why, don't you usually?' queried the now intrigued inspector.

'Yeah, but not my left hand.'

'What do you mean?'

'Well, the teacher said if you knew the answer you had to put your right hand up, and if you didn't know the answer you had to put your left hand up.'

Perhaps you'd better not try it. But actually an old colleague of mine did try it and on one question everybody put their left hand up. Yup, that meant nobody knew the answer. I asked him, 'What did you do?' He replied, 'I just said, "Yeah, right, good. Well, you all obviously know the answer to that so let's move on to the next one, shall we?"'

Practical exercise

Develop a reflective element for your school's planner to help pupils to reflect on what they have learned. Begin the process with a presentation about boys and reflection to a whole-staff meeting. Follow up in departmental meetings. Prepare a draft and do a trial.

Within the Breakthrough Programme (see Chapter 26), many schools devised these and found them massively useful. Few, however, got it right the first time. At the first draft stage, what teachers discovered was they were simply listing what they'd done, rather than what they'd learned and their views on what they'd learned.

Chapter 16
Writing

> **Overview**
> - 'Right boys – it's time to write': what are the issues with boys and writing?
> - Three things to avoid:
>   - Writing as punishment
>   - Copying from boards
>   - Criticising their handwriting – it's not their fault

Shortly after I'd left life in the classroom, I did all kinds of interesting things – I started reading books about education, as you don't get too much time to read books about education when you're delivering education (although as you can see, my books are quite quick and easy to read so do have a look at the others!), and I also began seriously to reflect on my life in the classroom. On one particular occasion, I sat down and started to put together a list of things that boys might say to me, on a bad day, when I wanted to get them to write. Then I wrote it out as a poem (because when I was nine, a teacher told me I could write poems, remember, and I've been writing them ever since).

> 'Right boys – time to write.'
> 'Sir, do we have to? Again?'
> 'Can't we just talk about it instead?'
> 'Sir, can I borrow a pen?'
> 'Can I have some paper, sir?
> I left my book at home last night.'
> 'How do you start?'
> 'How much do you have to write?'
> 'What if you don't finish?'
> 'Do you write on both sides of the sheet?'
> 'Does the spelling matter?'
> 'Does it have to be neat?'

> *'Do you have to copy out the question?'*
> *'Can't we just have a rest?'*
> *'My arm hurts, sir. I've got cramp.'*
> *'Do I have to copy it out in best?'*
> *'Can I go and work in the library?'*
> *'Can I do it on a computer instead?'*
> *'Sir, do I have to read it through?*
> *I know what it is I said.'*
> *'You're not gonna read it out, are you?'*
> *'I don't want it displayed.'*
> *'What's it for? Does it count?*
> *Is it part of our final grade?'*
>
> *Gary Wilson*

Any of these sound familiar? At a twilight session in a secondary school recently, one teacher said, 'I heard all those this afternoon.' Good day, eh?

Act

You might like to read this out loud at a department meeting. Read with energy and have fun with voices. How many do colleagues recognise? Then look together at what they are really saying using the notes below to help.

What are the boys *really* saying about writing?

So, what are the boys in this poem saying (not that they need much in the way of translation!)? Let's work through the poem, line by line.

'Right boys – time to write.'

This is a sentence we rarely deliver with great enthusiasm whilst the boys are sitting there bristling with excitement.

'Sir, do we have to? Again?'

Does there always have to be a catch at the end? We've seen them gradually lose interest as they get towards the end of a lesson because they know there's a catch coming. A primary teacher once told me that she overheard a couple of boys in the playground. One said to the other, 'Don't go near t' rabbits; she'll have you writing about 'em.'

'Can't we just talk about it instead?'

Boys generally enjoy discussion and certainly, if there was a choice between writing or discussion, it would be discussion that came at the top of every straw poll.

'Sir, can I borrow a pen?' / 'Can I have some paper, sir? I left my book at home last night.'

As secondary teachers we're all familiar with stalling techniques, which could of course be related to disorganisation!

'How do you start?'

While this might appear to be another time-wasting ploy, it's actually a fairly common and largely genuine plea. Unless sufficient time has been spent in class discussion, group discussion, debate, role play or hot-seating, a lot of boys simply can't put pen to paper and genuinely don't know where to start.

'How much do you have to write?'

Just how excited are those thousands of boys at the prospect of putting pen to paper when they ask this question? But then I do remember from my dim and distant past, hearing colleagues of mine, not me of course, saying (in a voice as miserable as sin), 'Right boys, I know you don't want to do this… I don't either really… but it's in the syllabus, so pick up your pens.' You can just see the boys, can't you? 'Great… I just can't wait.' (Cue slow motion fist pumps.)

Boys tell me all the time that they love teachers who love their jobs, who teach with enthusiasm. One nine-year-old boy said to me once, 'I love teachers who teach with passion!' Another told me, 'If teachers don't have a passion for their subject then how can they get us to be passionate about it?' It's true though, isn't it? If we're not teaching with enthusiasm most of the time, and with passion occasionally, then are we in the right job? There clearly are times when we're having to teach something that doesn't particularly excite us. I was working at the same conference as a primary teacher who announced as her opening gambit, 'I hate numeracy. I hate it! But I spend every day passionately pretending that I love it to bits.' So much that we have to do requires us to act the part. But when it comes to everything that we love about our chosen subject, how do we publicly express our passion?

> **Think**
>
> Do your boys know about your passion? How many of the following can you tick off in your classroom? How many might you do from now on?
>
> - ✓ A fabulous display of all that is wonderful about your subject.
> - ✓ A classroom library akin to a good bookshop's array of relevant works of non-fiction and, importantly, fiction that relates to your subject.
> - ✓ A 'wonderwall' that you constantly refresh, displaying (with their consent) brilliant pieces of original work from your classes.
> - ✓ Up-to-date news items related to your subject that may provoke animated conversations.
> - ✓ A stunning backcloth on your smartboard that will provide a challenge the minute pupils set foot through the door (Pobble 365 is a great source for this: www.pobble365.com).

'What if you don't finish?' / 'Do you write on both sides of the sheet?'

My exasperated response, and I'm not proud to admit it, would either be, 'No, when you've filled the page, carry on writing on the desk' or 'No, write down the edge of the paper next', neither of which are big or clever. They weren't funny then and they're not funny now (where's that lol emoji when you need it?!).

'Does the spelling matter?' / 'Does it have to be neat?'

Handwriting issues are not their fault. It's not their fault that boys were forced to write before they were physically ready to do so. Like other areas of development, the development of fine motor skills in many boys takes longer than in the majority of girls. It's not boys' fault that their handwriting is generally not as good… I've made a lot of boys feel better by telling them this. In fact, I've made many grown men feel better just by telling them this! When it comes to handwriting, good teachers will be sympathetic and understanding.

'Do you have to copy out the question?'

'No, it's a waste of life' is the correct answer.

'Can't we just have a rest?' / 'My arm hurts, sir. I've got cramp.' / 'Do I have to copy it out in best?'

Boys are not big fans of copying something out in best. In fact, as we'll see on page 111, copying things out, particularly from books and boards, is boys' number one hate. As for the pain in their arm, there's a reason for that, as we'll see on page 112.

> **What I'd like to see**
>
> '[I'd like to see] teachers being less harsh and critical about my writing.'
> 'Sometimes they need to give us more time to finish stuff off. When I'm trying real hard to write neat then it takes much longer and I run out of time in the lesson.'
> 'If I write slow and neat I don't finish all the questions in the exam, then it can affect my future.'

'Can I go and work in the library?'

'Anywhere but here. I can't stand being here, writing, which for me can be totally demoralising, with the teacher constantly looking over my shoulder with the occasional grimace. Not to mention the fact we have to do it in silence.' Having to work in silence is a top three hate for boys in secondary school. One boy said to me once, 'It's like being dead.'

'Can I do it on the computer instead?'

We all know that this will help reduce their frustration with the way their work looks. Their teachers' frustration too.

'Sir, do I have to read it through? / I know what it is I said.'

A very male thing, this one. For a lot of boys, to get them to look through their work for mistakes can be very difficult. To get them to look through someone else's work for mistakes, no problem! We call that peer assessment (apart from a group of schools I worked with recently who called it 'Pimp my write' – doesn't work for everybody!). Peer assessment is a significant element of the assessment for learning agenda, which could have been written with just boys in mind. A systematic approach suits boys, for example: 'Do this… do that… get there.'

Think

Look again at the assessment for learning and discuss with your department just how many of the elements can literally tick the boxes for boys.

'You're not going to read it out, are you?'

Of course we are! We can make it sound good, we can embellish it, edit it, give it some life. If we get them to read it out and they have got any issue with that, then it can be a crushing experience. According to research, in the UK, public speaking is our biggest fear. Number two is death! That's how significant it is. I reckon I have taught *Macbeth* probably 30 times but I only gave out parts around the room once, the first time, because they weren't following the plot or the rhythm of the piece. Most were constantly taking a sneaky peek at the text to find out when their next public humiliation was due. So, on the vast majority of occasions I would read the whole text (and many other texts too), every single word, myself.

'I don't want it displayed.'

I never thought to ask. I thought I was being wonderfully egalitarian displaying everybody's work. But it's essential to get a pupil's consent.

'What's it for? Does it count? / Is it part of our final grade?'

What have we done to them? Actually, it's not what have we done to them; it's… what have *they* made us do to them? For boys, most boys, seeing a sense and purpose in doing something will serve to engage them. Worst-case scenario? If the work is not part of their final assessment then it requires little to no effort.

Seeing the back of these three things would help

If we're trying to positively engage boys in writing then we have to address three issues to begin with, which still seem to rear their ugly heads with alarming regularity: giving writing as punishment, copying out and criticising their handwriting.

Giving writing as punishment

See page 66 for more on this.

> **What I'd like to see**
>
> 'I'd like an end to being given writing as punishment.'

> **Act**
>
> Stop doing this – now!

Getting them to copy things from books or from boards

Boys can be at their most articulate (!) when talking about copying things from books and from boards. A significant proportion of writing in secondary schools is copied from the board or from books. As far as boys are concerned, having to copy from books and from boards is 'a waste of life' and 'a waste of trees'! One Year 7 boy said to me once, 'And we're supposed to be an eco school.' Other comments about this include:

- 'Copying out means it's not being interpreted into your own language. And when you come to look at it again for revision or whatever, you don't understand it.'
- 'It doesn't engage you. It doesn't help you.'
- 'It's repetitive.'
- 'It's not learning.'
- 'It just makes it look like you've done loads of work but realistically they've just put a PowerPoint on and asked you to copy it.'
- 'You don't read it; you're just copying shapes down onto your page, and sometimes the teacher moves on too fast and you miss out a bit, but it doesn't matter, 'cos you're never gonna read it again.'

When I ask why they think teachers get them to do that stuff, they say, 'It's because they can't be bothered to teach us' or as one boy put it, 'It's because the teacher can't be arsed.' Another said, 'They obviously know we hate it because sometimes the teacher will threaten us with having to just sit there in silence and copy things out.' A double whammy (triple if you count having to sit in silence – 'It's like being dead').

> **Act**
>
> How about you? Do a monitoring exercise of the amount of copying that goes on in school. It may surprise you. Asking the group in front of you to copy a chunk of work in English period 5, when they have (unbeknownst to you) had to copy a chunk out in French period 4, history period 3, religious studies

> period 2, and maths period 1, may be a step too far. Add to that the fact that one or two of them have been kept behind to copy out the school's lofty aims a hundred times. How is that boy's attitude towards writing just now? Take a tip from tens of thousands of boys and significantly reduce the amount of copying out, with a view to completely phasing it out.

Criticising their handwriting

'Here we are, struggling to write, whilst the girls race ahead with their neat and swirly writing,' one 11-year-old told me. It's not their fault. How many men do you know who have developed a fine, beautiful cursive handwriting of which they feel very proud right through to adulthood? How many men do you know, on the other hand, who were surrounded by girls all the way through school and were constantly told, 'Mmm, that's lovely and neat, dear' and the teacher has just grimaced at their work and moved on? The reason? Because we continue, against the advice of many, to force boys to write before they are physically ready to do so. It is generally accepted that, on average, girls develop the fine motor skills needed for writing at a younger age than boys do. My advice to the government and anybody else who would care to listen is this: if you want to continue seeing boys underachieve then carry on doing this, carry on forcing them to read and write before they are physically and mentally able to do so, because that's what you've been doing for a very long time.

Act

> Be kind and supportive about boys' handwriting, remarking positively at the slightest improvement. Go for quality over quantity and content over presentation. Cut them some slack and see the change.

When I talk to four- and five-year-old boys about writing, they don't say, 'It's those subjunctive clauses that are throwing me' (no, we don't do those until they're six, do we?!). No, they say it hurts. 15- and 16-year-old boys tell me the same thing, 'It hurts', and we know why, don't we? It's because so many of them were forced to write before they were physically ready to do so. Many then had to face the gladiatorial arena that was the pen licence. You know the thing: if you can wield a pencil effectively enough then you can have a pen. I met a 75-year-old man the other day who was still writing in pencil (kidding, but I do encounter countless parents who have had negative experiences of pen licences with their own boys).

Working in a London borough recently, I held two discussion groups with 20 eight-year-old boys. One of the questions I asked, gingerly, was: 'How many of you have got a pen licence?' One boy's hand shot up immediately. 'They're just for girls them, sir!' he bellowed. In another group of 20 boys, one boy put his hand up and said, 'I've got a pen licence, sir. It's because a teacher gave me a special PenAgain pen last year.' (Other pens and pencils are available. In fact, there are dozens of differently designed writing implements – get some in!)

We've known about making sure that we use the right kind of writing implement for a long time, in fact, a very long time. At a loose end, with time on my hands in Salisbury, I went to seek out the Magna Carta, as you do. It is to be found in Salisbury Cathedral. It's a tiny wee document. My first impression was 'But… there are no paragraphs!' (once an English teacher, always an English teacher), but there was a note next to it explaining that the reason for every single square centimetre being covered was because a piece of vellum that size, in those days, was worth the equivalent of two weeks' wages. So, I thought, fair enough, and pocketed my red pen. But more interestingly, a note, accompanying two quills, laid side by side to emphasise the subtle differences, revealed that a scribe who was right-handed would use a quill from the left wing of a particular bird whilst a left-handed scribe would best be served by using a quill from the right wing. We've known about making sure that we use the right kind of writing implement for years but I'm not sure we've taken enough notice of the fact.

There are countless boys who have not achieved a pen licence by the end of primary school or even had their licences revoked because they couldn't maintain their neat writing or for a myriad of other reasons. One parent told me her son was so upset that he hadn't achieved a pen licence by the end of Year 5 that she decided to make a joke of it: 'Let's see if we can get right to the end of Year 6 without getting it, eh? Let's go for it, eh?' Another parent told me that her five-year-old son's Christmas wish was that the Christmas elves would take away all the pens and pencils so that he wouldn't have to write any more. I hear from significant numbers of parents of the impact the pen licence, or lack of, has had or is having on their boys, not to mention the mother who remarked at a parents' session that her husband was still upset about never having gained a pen licence at school. He was 32.

The most marks you can lose for poor handwriting at GCSE? Between one and three, depending on the subject. What learners mostly stand to lose is an awful lot of self-esteem and confidence from the age of four or five, as it is our tendency as parents and as professionals alike to focus on the way their work looks. And it's not their fault. Worst-case scenario? Imagine a boy, whose handwriting has been an issue with, shall we say, one particular teacher, and that same teacher has constantly been saying throughout the GCSE years, 'They've got to be able to read it, you know, they've got to be able to read it!' That boy will have that voice going through his head over and over again and will maybe write so slowly that he only gets two thirds of the way through the paper. The sadness is that those of us, like myself, who marked

English papers for aeons (for me 27 years – we had to or there'd be no holidays) can read the drunken rantings of an ant dipped in ink because that's what we're paid to do. I can't remember ever returning a single script because I couldn't read it. That's not the issue. The issue is not to lose sight of the fact that in many cases, if we focus on the way it looks in a negative way, it cuts him to the very quick. It is part of his self-image and he would almost certainly prefer for his work to be beautifully neat, but just constantly reminding him of his inability to write neatly will not lead to any kind of improvement.

Act

Make sure, when you're looking over his shoulder watching him writing, that making a negative comment about his handwriting isn't the first thing you do. In fact, don't mention it at all until you've got time to talk quietly and sensibly about it.

If you do have the chance to talk quietly and sensibly to him about his writing, then back this up with:

- **Providing a selection of writing implements for him to try:** Pens of any kind or pencils, dammit. Why not?
- **Five minutes' practice:** A handwriting expert once told me that a very simple way of bringing about some speedy changes was to encourage making circular shapes equal and sticky-up bits equal. Ask him to try this before starting a piece of homework.
- **Before he sits down to do an extended piece of writing, an exam or whatever, get him to limber up!** For example, he could screw up an A4 sheet of scrap paper into a tiny, tiny ball in his writing hand, then straighten it out again using the same hand. You wouldn't dream of playing a sport without warming up the muscles you're going to use. (At one time I started a booklet of these exercises with a sports science lecturer friend. We were going to call it 'hand gym', until we suddenly thought that adolescent boys would have had far too much fun with that title.)
- **Make doubly sure that he writes in black ink:** As examination papers are now scanned prior to marking, the two handwriting issues that have come up from markers is colour of ink and size of writing. Any colour other than black will not make a clear enough scan; neither does tiny handwriting. (At the time of writing it was still open to examiners to ask for the original script. This was barely done at all.)

Practical exercise

Prepare an action plan on getting it right for boys with writing across the curriculum, which clearly shows that they have been listened to. Monitor and celebrate small successes. Share them as a staff.

One really effective way of moving things forward is by utilising the PDSA model, the main strategy of the National Education Breakthrough Programme established by the (then) NHA and supported by the DfES Innovations Unit. The PDSA model can be tried out and tested by just one person, a whole subject area, the pastoral team or the senior leadership team.

P represents **planning** a simple strategy, for example a 'revision breakfast' the morning of an exam. **D** represents **doing** it. **S** is for **studying** the strategy in action and then **A** is **assessing** the effectiveness of the strategy. If it works, pass it on; if it doesn't then bin it. It may need modifying before wider dissemination. It's vital, of course, that successes and failures are shared as a whole staff.

Chapter 17
Reading

> **Overview**
> - Boys' attitudes to reading pre-secondary school
> - Libraries and boys' reading
> - Why boys need to read fiction
> - Promoting reading
> - Linking up with your primaries
> - Holding exciting literature-based events in your library
> - Sharing *your* passion
> - Using older boys as role models (especially peer leaders)
> - It's not just about reading for pleasure – it's about reading test papers too!

'I've never read a book, ever.'

I've heard the above phrase more than once. A secondary English teacher for almost 30 years, I spent a lot of that time simply assuming that all boys loved reading in primary school. Actually, I was wrong. A lot of boys begin primary school thinking that reading is a girly thing to do. Why? Largely, I would suggest, it is because they may never be read to by a man at home. As we saw on page 29, boys may never see a man around the house reading, and if they do, they may only ever see us reading the newspaper or an instruction manual. I also mentioned that the most recent figures from the Book Trust (2020) suggest that only 37 per cent of children up to the age of nine are read to at home, and the received wisdom is that quite a proportion of those are only read to by mums.

Libraries in secondary schools are often packed full with boys at lunchtimes, but they're mostly not reading. They're seeking sanctuary away from what we used to call the 'killing ground' in the sixties. I wrote the poem on the following page about this situation.

I love the library
It's my special place
I love the library
It's warm and it's safe
I love the library
It's the playground I fear
I love the library
They can't get me here
I love the library
I love the way it looks
I love the library
But I can't stand books

Gary Wilson
(*From* Breaking Through Barriers to Boys' Achievement)

Common responses from so many boys in secondary schools when you ask them about reading include: 'I used to read in primary school, because you had to there.' Another boy replied, 'Yeah and you used to get points for that and I loved that.' One boy, typical of countless others, told me, 'I only read when I have to. I don't read anything else.' When I ask a group, 'What stopped you reading?', I get responses ranging from 'I grew up!' to 'Real life got in the way. I've got far more to do with my time now' and 'I'd rather watch stuff.'

And it doesn't help when, as with writing, I regularly hear comments such as: 'They always make you read when you're in isolation. Now I guess I associate reading with punishment.'

Think

Consider the following questions:

- What could you do as a school to help those who did love reading in primary school to maintain their interest in reading during their transition to secondary?
- What do you do for the boys who gave up reading for pleasure early into their time at secondary school?
- How do we get them to reignite their interest?

Reading fiction

All boys would massively benefit from reading and, specifically, reading fiction. The old stereotype – 'let them read whatever they're interested in (usually referred to here are non-fiction texts, such as books of records, football club annuals and books on dinosaurs or aliens); they'll move on to the other stuff eventually' – doesn't hold water. It is widely understood that there are many boys in secondary schools who hardly ever read for pleasure at all. What's more, if you dip into non-fiction as a beginner reader, you fail faster because most of it is significantly harder to read. A study involving 45,000 students in the USA showed that girls tend to read more fiction, particularly in high school. It is well understood that reading challenge levels tend to be higher for non-fiction than fiction. Pupils who read a greater proportion of non-fiction made less reading progress than pupils who read a high proportion of fiction.

Boys generally provide lower estimations of their reading abilities than girls do:

- Boys value reading as an activity less than girls do.
- Boys have much less interest in leisure reading than girls do, and are far more likely to read for utilitarian purposes than girls are.
- Significantly more boys than girls declare themselves to be non-readers.
- Boys express less enthusiasm for reading than girls do. (Smith and Wilhelm, 2002)

Why fiction?

Fiction exposes children to a wide range of experiences, attitudes and people that mirror real life. Fiction aids understanding of what others think and feel and do. When identifying with characters and their emotions, boys begin to understand their own emotions and those of others. Fiction gives them strategies to deal with dilemmas and conflicts. Stories of famous people and heroes can illustrate perseverance, hard work and determination in overcoming obstacles. Above all, fiction gives them the words with which to express themselves. It is in fiction where boys will find the words to help them unclench their hearts.

As a head of English, I used to ban non-fiction during that precious single period of free reading we managed to shoehorn into the school day for Years 7, 8 and 9. Why? I got fed up of them charging into the library and fighting over *The Guinness Book of Records*. There'd be blood on the pages. They'd start flicking from the back to the front then front to middle to back, then after five minutes of flicking they'd swap it for *The History of Manchester United* or some such, and after five minutes of further flicking they'd swap that for *The Twits* or *The Magic Finger*, something they'd read when they were four or five, in case the teacher came round and asked them about the story they'd been reading.

How to get boys reading fiction

In the secondary school library, for example, you could have a special promotion of books that boys might enjoy. To begin with, this could be fiction related to their interests, including TV and film tie-ins, graphic novels (these are fine as at least they are reading chronologically), and books with male characters who they can relate to.

Many years ago, I was working as a head of English in a school which displayed a remarkable similarity to the school in Barnsley where the film version of *Kes* (otherwise known as *A Kestrel for a Nave*) was shot. *Kes* was head and shoulders above any other book in terms of popularity with the boys. It was also one of only a handful of things they didn't mind reading around the class, as everyone was desperately hoping their page or paragraph would have a swear word on it that they could read aloud with gusto: 'Come on Billy, gerrup! Hands off cocks on socks!' or 'You're a bastard.' It was also the book that was stolen in significant numbers every year. I had no problem with that. I knew for a fact that in some cases it became the only book in their homes.

An approach that can reap rich rewards for both groups involved is the fairly common practice of working cross phase on fairly small-scale literacy projects. Link up with a feeder primary school and ask if they would like some of your boys to go down to read to some pupils. Include in your selection of boys the most reticent readers for this. They will need to be trained first, of course, in how to communicate the joy and power of reading.

> **What I'd like to see**
>
> 'I remember when I was in Year 1, some boys from the big school came down to read stories to us. It was really great.'
> 'Yeah and one time they even wrote stories especially for us with us in… I was in a book!'

These are the kinds of things that they never forget. Typically I would use this idea as a focus for a piece of GCSE coursework. We'd go down to one of our feeder primaries and they would talk to the little ones about the kind of stories they liked. One or two would lose interest after a while and wander off and play in the water or the sandpit. The little ones would too. (Just kidding!) We'd go away and over a couple of weeks produce wonderful storybooks, paying particular attention to presentation, as the school would be expecting copies for their school library. The day we went down, the boys were surprisingly nervous, but the little ones really made them welcome, they gave them orange juice and they made them biscuits. The big boys read them their stories, they drank their orange juice, ate their biscuits, and returned to school, delighted with their efforts and the reception they received. On more than one occasion we'd got a letter from the children at the local school, saying: 'We've writ some stories now for your big boys. Can we bring them up?' You can imagine their 'books', two or three drawings stapled together. Their characters' body shapes with various limbs sticking out at random with a couple of words scribbled underneath. But the boys were absolutely thrilled. There was a pause in the celebration when one boy suddenly realised, 'Oh no, we're going to have to learn how to make biscuits'!

To extend this into their own homes, encourage them to read their stories to their younger siblings. Also have a selection of high-quality children's picture books in your library that pupils can be encouraged to take home to read to their younger siblings. Particularly useful are books that appeal to any age, including books by Shaun Tan, the 'Oi Frog' series and children's books by Roald Dahl, the Ahlbergs and Julia Donaldson, and the old classics such as *Winnie the Pooh* and *Alice in Wonderland*.

Think about what you are doing as, for example, a history, geography or science teacher with regard to pointing boys in the direction of historical novels, travel stories or science fiction. How might you develop a project for your subject area in conjunction with your school librarian? If such reading is your passion, what can you do to show pupils that you are a passionate reader of, for example, all things historical?

Think

Consider the following questions:

- Does the librarian work closely with the heads of all departments to select books that would fit the bill for the above?
- Is your library the living heart of the school?
- Have you got a fully functioning library?
- Is there open access to your library all day, every day?

Literature-based activities

Desperate to engage more boys in the library many years ago, I decided to introduce a whole series of literature-based activities. One of my favourites was one I introduced around the time of the first *Lord of the Rings* films. Around the same time, a wonderful model emporium called the Games Workshop started to sell beautifully crafted miniature elves, orcs, hobbits and the like for table-top reenactments of battles and other scenes. I paid a visit to one of their wonderful emporiums. For those who may never have visited, their shops are filled to the rafters with tiny lead and plastic models and the assistants tend to be bearded and garbed all in black. They'll come up to you as you peruse the giant table that is adorned with a beautifully intricate battle scene and in a deep breathy voice intone, 'We've got a new line in elves if you're interested.' So, I invited them into school to run a lunchtime workshop in the school library. The day arrived, as did two bearded visitors, dressed in black (with their new line in elves and much more), who immediately set about creating a wonderful battle scene on a board that was larger than four tables. The boys immediately became totally engrossed as a reenactment of the flight to the ford unfolded before their very eyes. Fascinated, I noticed that around the table was a massively diverse group, many of whom had hardly set foot in the library. But here they were, actively engaged with an activity that required a decent knowledge of a classic work of literature and also significant literacy skills that enabled them to navigate rule books as thick as a telephone directory.

This seemed to me to be a great example of what can happen when you give them something related in some way to your subject that motivates and excites them – they will engage.

Give them positive experiences of reading

It's worth noting that if a struggling reader or a reticent reader *always* has to write about something they've just read, we're adding another hurdle – giving them another reason to reject reading. It isn't normal, is it? As a primary colleague of mine suggested at a literacy conference we were both speaking at, always having to do something, to write something, to make something after reading something is not natural behaviour: 'If I finish reading a book in bed with my husband, I don't go down to the kitchen and make a diorama. It's not natural!' It is important that boys who are reluctant to read have successful reading experiences. Small mixed-ability groups can provide the kind of support they need. They can talk to others in meaningful ways about the books they have read or are reading. Small groups are best, and friendship groups are possibly the easiest way to set up these discussions.

Be a reading role model

'Male teacher-librarians (particularly) need to read books – lots of books. Always have a book on hand. Carry it. Know a wide selection of books that boys will read. Always be ready to talk to boys about what's good. Listen to them to learn who they are and what they want so you can motivate them – move them – from where they are to the next level, wherever that might be for that particular reader. Share your passion for reading and never stop reading, talking and sharing.' (Shoemaker, 2003)

You can make a difference on this basis. Share your passion for reading and model what you do as a reader – talk about books to other readers. Never say you're not into reading, you prefer films, you haven't got time or it's boring (even if it's true!). Also try the following:

- ✓ Be an advocate, following pupils' reading journeys when time permits – in tutor time, for example.
- ✓ Recommend books that you read or that your children read.
- ✓ Have a 'I'm currently reading…' sign on your classroom door.
- ✓ Have a recommended reads section on your school website.
- ✓ Have a comic or graphic novel club.
- ✓ Have a reading challenge for all from Year 7 onwards.
- ✓ Display and promote subject-related fiction in subject-specific classrooms, for example, science fiction in science labs, historical novels in history, and so on.
- ✓ Display pictures of staff from all subject areas engaged in reading.

Act

Try compiling a list called '16 books to read before you're 16'. This is a great subject for Changemakers (see Chapter 24, page 155) to research with teachers and pupils.

I always recommend that you use your own boys as positive role models in posters and displays. I dearly love the National Literacy Trust, the organisation that has done more than any other in the realms of engaging boys in reading. I'm sure they'll forgive me for this, but about 15 years ago, they first ran a poster campaign to motivate boys to read. The posters included sportsmen, including a footballer who was reading his book upside down, and – wait for it – Alan Titchmarsh reading. I was working in a fairly challenging school at the time, and when that particular poster arrived, I thought, 'I can just see it now. Wicked! (Finger snap.) If he reads a book, lead me to a bookshop!' I didn't put it up. But I did start a poster campaign myself that included key players, such as PE teachers, the peer police from Year 10 (see page 71), boys from that tricky Year 8 cohort, ex-pupils, and so on.

Act

Devise a campaign in conjunction with a small group of pupils to engage and motivate boys with their reading, using reading challenges, 'extreme reading', subject-specific displays in the library on a rota basis (primary schools are brilliant at this) and multimedia presentations (maybe including YouTube-type presentations) devised by pupils working with staff.

> **Think**
>
> What are you already doing to encourage boys who are reticent readers to read? What else might you do? (You could stop reading being given as punishment for a start.) What do you already do out of the suggestions mentioned in this chapter? What else could you do?

It's not just about reading for pleasure

In case we were in any doubt about the significant value of reading beyond the act of reading books for pleasure, consider the fact that more than half the mistakes that boys make in tests and exams are because they misread the question. If only we could get that bit right! We know from our own experience, or even from a cursory glance at the issue, that those boys who do read tend to read far more non-fiction than girls do. That's OK, you may say; at least they're reading. A huge study of 800,000 pupils undertaken by Keith Topping (2017) showed that boys of all ages were indeed choosing non-fiction but boys are not reading non-fiction as carefully or as thoroughly as girls were reading non-fiction. They take less time to process the words, often skipping parts. And they choose books that are too easy, instead of moving on to tougher material. Topping said, 'What they are doing is not particularly good – and they are lagging behind.' Topping's suggestion, as we have explored above, is to make every effort we can to engage boys with reading by finding books that interest boys and which are challenging in order to keep them focused on the page.

Practical exercise

Deploy a group of boys (such as the Changemakers – see Chapter 24, page 155) in a piece of research into reading habits that they can report back to the whole school. If you have the software in school that allows you to ascertain the age and gender of library users, that would make a decent starting point.

Chapter 18
What makes a good lesson

> **Overview**
> - Practical lessons – trust me to do things!
> - Making it memorable
> - Taking breaks
> - Working in groups and having discussions

All the boys I've ever asked about what makes a good lesson share remarkably similar ideas, some of which I've summed up in this poem:

'A good lesson starts at the classroom door
With a smile, not a frown from the lesson before.'
'S' about being sat next to your best mate,
So if you don't understand he can translate.'
'It's not having to work in silence –
That's like being dead.'
'A good lesson's for having a laugh instead
Having a laugh – knowing when enough's enough?'
'It's when you don't have to write or worse, copy out stuff.'
'It's when a teacher doesn't scream and shout'
'And doesn't call you names.
Or order you out.'
'Or put the class in detention
When only one was to blame
When only one was to blame and it wasn't you.'
'A good lesson for me
And a good lesson for you?'

Gary Wilson

Practical lessons

Popular is the kind of lesson where the teacher guides you through the lesson, and doesn't just say, after a brief introduction, "Right, now get on with it!"' However, boys like it when this direct instruction is balanced with 'doing things'. Unpopular is a lesson dominated by having to complete work on a worksheet, but popular are more practical lessons where pupils are trusted to do things and given responsibility. One boy told me a good lesson is when 'you're involved – when there's more interactivity'. Another boy referred to something I regularly encounter, when a class or group is told in science, for example, when they are bursting to do more practical work, 'You're not to be trusted – you can copy down from the board instead.'

> **What I'd like to see**
>
> 'I'd like to be trusted more to do things and be given responsibility.'

Making it memorable

You can't imagine them sitting around with their own classmates in ten years' time going, 'Do you remember that worksheet that we did in January 2020?' So make it memorable! Make the work feel like it's not work.

> **Think**
>
> Given a choice, would they come to your lessons?

Taking breaks

Having short breaks is a popular idea. It's not rocket science, as we know. I asked a young lad once, 'How can teachers improve your lessons?' He responded, quick as a flash, with a face twisted in anguish, 'I just wish they'd let me get up now and again.' Not a lot to ask.

Group work and discussions

Boys do favour group work, and as far as most are concerned, they don't do enough. Discussions are another important point. After every discussion I have with boys regarding their achievement, I always ask if they have enjoyed the session, to which the answer is almost invariably yes, they have. I ask if they enjoy discussions in lessons to which the normal response is mostly that they hardly ever do them at all.

> **What I'd like to see**
>
> 'I'd like more discussions in class. We don't do any. Until you're in trouble that is. Then there's a discussion.'

It all comes down to the teacher

Whether boys will think your lesson is good or not will ultimately come down to the relationship you have with them as their teacher. Think about how well you get on with them, how you communicate with them and how you teach them. Boys tell me that good lessons depend on:

- ✓ 'How well you get on with the teacher.' (The most common response.)
- ✓ 'Whether teachers talk to you as though you're a real person.'
- ✓ 'How the teacher chooses to teach.'
- ✓ 'How the teacher stimulates your brain.'

What do teachers think?

In discussion with many teachers about what, in their opinion, helps boys succeed, the responses are always along the lines of when we:

- ✓ **Give them responsibility** – including Year 11s buddy reading with children from your feeder primaries (see page 15).
- ✓ **Give them a challenge** – preferably the minute they set foot in the classroom (see page 132).
- ✓ **Allow them to take the lead in their own learning**.
- ✓ **Engage them in active experiences** – from role play to outdoor learning.
- ✓ **Relate to things that interest them** – this is the basis of positive relationships, on a one-to-one basis, as a group or whole class.
- ✓ **Give them the chance to influence and determine activities** – giving them the opportunity to take the lead in their learning means their motivation will increase and so too will the quality of their outcome.

- ✓ **Value their experiences and make them feel like they are the experts**.
- ✓ **Give them lots of praise** – praise, praise and more praise – always specific, never phoney (see page 55).

Good lessons: a checklist

We tick a lot of boxes as far as boys are concerned when lessons:

- ✓ contain the opportunity for discussions
- ✓ relate to their interests in some way
- ✓ involve 'doing'
- ✓ include a choice of form for presenting their ideas
- ✓ include credit or rewards for doing well
- ✓ include having some fun (but not too much! Boys need boundaries. They need to know who's in charge, what the rules are and whether they are being applied consistently)
- ✓ don't include copying from books or boards
- ✓ sometimes include having music on ('It makes me work harder and faster, like when I'm on my bike!')
- ✓ are broken up with activities like multiple choice questions and quizzes
- ✓ include being asked to share their opinions.

Practical exercise

Engage with your department, pastoral team or senior leadership team in a discussion around what you believe brings out success in boys. Using your ideas (and any from the list above that you agree with), decide what you feel are the top five ways, in your combined experience, of helping boys to succeed. How often do you personally actively promote those approaches? Every day? Hardly at all?

Chapter 19
What can help

> **Overview**
>
> - Giving them the big picture
> - Turning them into lean mean revision machines
> - Challenge, not competition
> - Praise
> - Genuine human interest
> - Ask the experts

When I'm visiting a school, I find it really useful when I get a tour around the school conducted by pupils. On one such occasion, I asked a couple of Year 11 boys to show me places in the school that meant something special to them. The first place they took me to was the dining room. Immediately I smelt a rat (not literally, of course; that would have been even more disturbing). Thinking that they were intent on having a laugh at my expense, I said, 'All right boys, maybe I should just look around by myself!' They replied, 'No sir, wait sir. We've brought you here because we actually help design the nutritional balance of the meals that we have and the photographs (above the servery) are our work as well.' Suitably placated, not to mention a little embarrassed, I ushered them along to the next port of call, the design technology area, where we stood together silently contemplating two huge displays of coursework on opposite walls. In the corner of one of the displays was a gigantic A* and in the corner of the other a giant C. 'OK boys, impressive. Why is this important to you?' They said, 'Well sir, we wouldn't know what an A* looked like unless we'd seen this.' It made perfect sense. Boys do need to see the big picture.

And that's just one area that boys tell us to focus on to help with their education. So, to round off this part of the book, I'm going to summarise five key areas that boys tell us specifically can help them in school, before in Chapter 20, summarising three things that many schools are currently doing that boys tell us *don't* help. If you want a starting point for raising boys' achievement in your school, this may be it.

Giving boys the big picture

There's a reason why the big picture is so important for boys. Around about the age of five or six, boys tend to develop a right hemisphere dominance, which means they like, indeed they need, to see the big picture. It's precisely why, for example, graphic organisers can be particularly useful for many boys. If you think it would be useful to know more about how this impacts the boys in your school, so that you may guide them effectively when it comes to revision, for example, here are some questions you might like to ask the boys:

- Does it help to know exactly why you are following a particular line of enquiry?
- Does it help to know the big picture so that you can see where what you're about to do fits in with what you're doing at the moment?
- What do you think about checklists?
- What about learning mats?
- Mindmaps?
- Graphic organisers?
- Is there anything else that you find helpful?

Turning them into lean mean revision machines

I often ask small groups of boys, 'Boys, what is your preferred revision style?' The first answer I usually get is, 'You what?' I rephrase it, 'How do you revise?'
'I read my notes.'
'And then what do you do?'
'I read them again.'
'And then what do you do?'
'I read them again.'
'And then?'
'Then I fall asleep!'
To this, you want to say, 'Well you will do, won't you, because that's not the best way for you to revise, is it?' The variety found in interactive programmes including Bitesize, SAM Learning and Quizlet, for example, is crucial. As we know, encouraging pupils to make their own revision resources can help, as can breaking up their own revision notes with illustrations, bullet points, mind maps and other graphic organisers, such as Venn diagrams. Quizzing with friends or parents can help too. Variety and movement are key. Some of you may remember the hope, often expressed, that once we saw the back of coursework then the gender gap would begin to close,

based on the assumption that doing exams suited boys far better, since the major issue with regard to boys and coursework was that many left it until the very last minute. In some subjects, we were giving them their coursework in, say, October and telling them it was to be submitted in February. When were a lot of the boys starting that then, eh? February, I hear you say. (Good school; a lot of people say March.) Then we improved matters by saying, 'Here's the first chunk you have to deliver.' We gave them the criteria they had to meet and the deadline a month hence. Then we gave them feedback, fast and furious, then set the next month's chunk, and so on and so on. Boy-friendly chunks. Big bywords when it comes to most boys.

But, of course, the end of coursework didn't lead to the closing of the gap. That didn't happen. Why? Because there's not just one reason why boys are failing to achieve as well as girls.

What it does mean though now is that boys need to become, like so many of their female counterparts already are, lean revision machines. It will have escaped not a single teacher's, pupil's or parent's notice that if you're doing eight or nine GCSEs, you're doing the best part of 30 exams. The first year this happened, so many teachers complained to me how ridiculous it was that students may have a three-hour written exam in the morning, followed by another two-hour written exam in the afternoon.

> **Think**
>
> Are we teaching them a wide range of revision strategies from Year 7 from which they can choose those strategies that will serve them best? What else could we do?

Challenge, not competition

Whenever anyone strikes up a conversation with me about my work, be it a taxi driver, a parent who is worried about their boy, a nurse administering a blood test or a dentist examining my teeth, they say, 'I bet you use competition to get those boys working hard, don't you? 'Cos boys love competition, don't they though? Boys love competition… they do though, don't they, eh? They love competition.'

No, they don't.

Boys don't love competition. Where do we get that idea? Boys don't love competition. Boys who win competitions love competition, but those who don't win competitions, or barely do, rarely do or never do, they don't love competition. For them, it's a crushing experience every time it raises its ugly head. It's just something else for them to fail at, to feel bad about. But I've always thought this, haven't you? Not even fleetingly?

Other sources back me up on this. Carolyn Jackson (2006), Professor of Gender and Education at Lancaster University, writes 'Competitive practices create winners and losers and lead to defensive strategies by boys (and girls) to protect their self-image whereby they withdraw from competition rather than risk failure.' Similarly, psychologist Stephen Biddulph (2018) says, 'Competitiveness as a personality trait stems from compulsively searching for approval that never comes. Even winning, as many top athletes find, is not enough.'

So, no, boys do not love competition. But what boys do love is a challenge. We know they love a challenge. Don't they love it when you make a mistake on the smartboard? My advice? Make more mistakes, become totally incompetent. Say: 'I can't remember a single word of this story – you're going to have to remind me' or 'I've lost the written instructions for the battery tester' and wait for the response: 'I'll sort it for you, miss' or 'I'll sort it for you, sir!'

And what's more, as far as boys are concerned, they need a challenge the minute they set foot through the door, as often as possible. Research suggests that it's between ten and 12 minutes into a lesson before the first challenge appears (Hughes, 2002). Enough time for some boys to have almost totally disengaged. When it comes to presenting a challenge the minute children set foot in school, primary teachers are brilliant at it, grabbing their pupils' attention, arousing their interest and challenging them the minute they arrive. There are signs around the school that an alien spaceship has landed in the playground during the holidays. How else can they explain the four perfectly circular scorch marks on the field, slime sliding slowly down the window and the aliens' footprints in the glitter on the nursery floor? Why was the headteacher found tied up in the office first thing on Monday morning? Who knows, but the whole school population arrives not at school but at a crime scene where they need to start investigations straight away.

If not an alien landing in the secondary school (stretching the older ones' suspension of disbelief a little too far maybe) then at least try a little something to operate as a silent starter. At the time of writing, the free website Pobble 365 is a daily (the clue's in the title) source of the most staggering images that can stimulate their imaginations and spark great conversation. Their images are also brilliant for Philosophy for Children (P4C) sessions. But most useful of all, try a piece of problem-solving related to the work they're about to complete in the lesson.

Act

Have fun producing some short, problem-solving activities related to your subject, and even more specifically, related to the particular area of your subject that they are currently involved with. Or, how about finding some inspirational illustrations related to your subject and displaying them on your screen?

> **Think**
>
> If it feels relevant to you and your school, have that discussion about challenge versus competition with a colleague, with your department or with senior leaders. What are the implications for the house system, for example? You could reframe it as not an inter-house competition anymore, rather an inter-house challenge. It means that everyone's a winner if they have risen to the challenge and done their best.

Praise

Boys are very clear on this one. They like praise:

- 'If I've been told I'm doing good that changes everything.'
- 'What helps is when I've been told the positives.'
- 'If I had a bit more recognition for my work it would keep me a lot more engaged.'

> **❝ What I'd like to see**
>
> 'When I feel like I'm doing well in a subject or if I get told I'm working well in a subject, that makes a lot of difference. It changes the way I walk into the next lesson. I'm thinking, right, I'm doing well, I want to carry on doing well. If I'm told or made to feel like I'm not good at something then I have no motivation to work harder. What's helpful is when I've been praised.' ❞

With one group, I listed the kinds of rewards that boys seem to appreciate according to my research (see Chapter 7). At the mention of the most popular, one boy appeared to go into some kind of reverie… 'A positive phone call home would turn everything around. That would be amazing!' one Year 9 boy declared. His desire for such a thing was almost palpable.

As I mentioned in Chapter 7, we know that most boys seem to need more praise and encouragement than girls do. And we know why too. It's because they've attracted attention for mostly negative reasons since squat and we have to compensate for that. But the praise that we give them must be very specific to what it is that they've done. If you say, 'Errol, you're brilliant!', he'll have no idea why you're saying he's brilliant. Therefore, the chance of him repeating whatever it was will be very slim. If you say, 'I love the way you've blended together those colours to create the sea. That's really good', then he'll take it on board. The praise that we give him should never be phoney, and boys are onto phoney. Charlie hasn't put his hand up for ages, but today he has: 'Charlie, that was a stunning response!' Charlie knows it wasn't a stunning response and he won't be putting his hand up again for quite a while, thank you.

Genuine human interest

A group of Year 11s were fulsome in their praise of the system in their school where each pupil during the early stages of Year 11 met with a senior teacher in school to discuss their future. The headteacher made it very plain: 'We make it very clear to each and every one of them that we are not letting them go onto the next stage of their lives without having that proper grown-up conversation.'

I can honestly say that my experience of the work in the Breakthrough Programme with 150 secondary schools (see Chapter 26) taught me something hugely powerful. What made the difference for the vast majority of the boys who were being mentored was the fact that they just had that extra little bit of genuine human interest in them as individuals – as people.

Ask the experts

The above is just a starting point. As I've said throughout this book, the best next step for you is to ask the boys in your setting what you can do to help. Here are some tips for teachers from Oliver, aged 12:

- ✓ Treat every day as a new day.
- ✓ Say hello to everyone.
- ✓ Get to know our interests and include them in our work.
- ✓ Stop being cruelly humorous.
- ✓ Engage more in the corridor.
- ✓ Stop the 'man-up' stuff.
- ✓ Show me positivity.
- ✓ Stop escalating behaviour.
- ✓ Think about how it would be for you as a child.
- ✓ Do fun, eventful things that make me want to come back for more.

We know from boys what type of lesson suits them (see Chapter 18) and we understand what it is that they feel will help them succeed. So, let's do it, then!

Chapter 20
What doesn't help and what gets in the way

> **Overview**
> - Relationships: 'A teacher can really kill it or make it for you'
> - Injustices:
>   - 'Some teachers have their favourites'
>   - Treatment of boys versus treatment of girls
> - Being judged on reputation alone

In your experience, are boys even a tiny bit correct in any of the following descriptors?

- 'Not all teachers greet you as you come in.'
- 'And the thing is they carry the whole atmosphere of the class. I think it's important to start in a good mood.'
- 'Some teachers get on your back straight away – sometimes it's because of something that happened last lesson you had with them, and sometimes they're in a bad mood because of the lesson just before yours.'

These are remarkably common comments I get from boys in secondary schools. Poor relationships with teachers form a significant barrier that gets in the way of boys succeeding at school. In this chapter, we'll explore this further and look at some other common barriers that boys tell us really don't help their education, as well as what we can do to improve things.

Relationships

So much is to do with relationships:

- 'A teacher can really kill it or make it for you. I have a new English teacher and now I work really well.'
- 'I'm definitely less excited about working with some teachers than with others.'
- 'If you don't like the teacher, it makes the work twice as hard.'
- 'Yeah and some teachers stress you out.'
- 'Some teachers work with you, some work against you.'
- 'Some teachers are so strict you daren't ask a question.'
- 'Some teachers are just rude to you sometimes.'

> **Think**
>
> In your schooldays, who was the teacher you found least positive in their behaviour and attitude? Who was the most positive? What was the difference? Can you be the most positive? What would it take?

Boys want teachers who care about them and this starts with the basics: 'Sometimes a teacher's been teaching you for a year and they don't even know your name.' Sadly, a comment that is more and more typical of many groups of boys in recent years is: 'Some teachers just want the grades. They're not bothered about you.' Boys will be quick to spot good teaching as well, and this will make all the difference when it comes to a teacher's relationship with them:

- 'Some teachers put less effort in. They spend five minutes explaining something then they just hand out the textbooks and we have to just get on because you're expected to know it.'
- 'Sometimes you kind of know a teacher who hasn't planned the lesson well. And sometimes you end up doing work that you've done the week before.'

Injustices

'Some teachers have their favourites. I told one once. It didn't go down well.' In my experience, boys tend to be not only the best barometers of good teachers and good teaching, but also the best barometers of social injustice. Setting, as explored in Chapter 10, is for many the most significant area of injustice, closely followed by teachers having their favourites. This is exacerbated further by the differences boys perceive in how teachers treat boys and girls. In discussions, boys very often become more animated when they sense this perceived injustice than they do with most of the other issues:

- 'Some teachers often ignore girls' bad behaviour.'
- 'Boys get tugged around. Girls just get calmed down.'
- 'Some teachers trust girls more and are more likely to tell a boy off for talking.'
- 'I've got a deeper voice than everybody in my class which means it stands out and I get picked on for it.'
- 'If they have a go at some boys, their first instinct will be to have a go back. But girls will just back down.'

And on and on they go in the majority of discussions I've had with boys over the years, until I have to stop them when they start citing particular teachers by name.

> **What I'd like to see**
>
> 'Teachers need to treat boys and girls the same. I don't like how some teachers persecute boys and favour girls.'

Being judged on reputation

Linking to the idea of fairness, boys hate being judged on reputation alone, whether that's what has been said about them in the staff room, or even more unjustly, based on what other family members have done: 'What I hate is when teachers constantly compare me to my brother. We're like total opposites... It gets me down.' It can go even further back too. One boy told me, 'My dad's given me my reputation. Some of his teachers still teach here!' This can make boys feel that 'some teachers are out to get you.' Clearly, it is important that we give every boy a clean slate and don't let assumptions taint our relationship with him from the off.

Act

Surprise someone today who is always just under the radar by quietly saying something positive to him.

Part 3

Bringing it all together

Chapter 21
The problem with the problem with boys: getting teachers on board

> **Overview**
> - What *teachers* think about the barriers to boys' achievement
> - How does this compare to what the boys think?
> - Teachers make all the difference

On one occasion, before delivering a full day's training on boys' achievement in a secondary school, a headteacher asked if it would be OK if departments could first of all get their heads together for ten minutes to describe what the issues were around boys' achievement and what it was that was preventing them from succeeding. At the end of their animated discussions, the heads of department were asked to feed back. And so began a long litany of the failings and shortcomings of boys that were responsible for their failure in each individual department. Boys were underachieving, it was felt, because:

- They have low literacy levels for their work in humanities.
- There's some arrogance – boys think they're OK.
- They won't push themselves.
- They're disengaged.
- They do the bare minimum.
- They think we owe them high grades.
- They question our marking.
- The middle-set boys are apathetic.

- The bottom set lacks self-esteem.
- They disrupt others.
- They are too complacent.
- They have poor attitudes towards extra help.
- They create poor group dynamics.
- They lack motivation.
- They fear failure.
- They worry about their peers' perceptions.
- They need to raise their expectations.
- They lack organisation skills.
- They're childish.
- They need spoon-feeding.
- They lack any independent thoughts.
- They need to set themselves higher targets.
- The brightest ones have a lot of other things in their lives.
- They're disruptive.
- They're immature.
- They have no aspirations.
- They spend too much time trying to entertain others rather than work.
- They are loud-mouthed.
- They are disorganised.
- They are fidgety.
- They have a shorter concentration span.
- They are rude and disrespectful.
- They are untidy (and so is their work).
- They are restless.
- They don't listen.

And so on, and so on. Not one single department's feedback referred to anything that might even vaguely be construed as partly or wholly the responsibility of the teachers themselves. It was all about the boys. As the feedback ground to a halt, I quietly asked the head if I might start off with that observation as my opening gambit. With a grin, he replied, 'Go for it!'

The problem with the problem with boys: getting teachers on board 143

> **Think**
>
> How many of the statements on pages 141 and 142 could teachers help boys with?

Consider how these responses compare to what we've heard the boys say throughout this book when asked the same question: 'Describe what the issues are around boys' achievement and what it is that is preventing some boys from succeeding.' Ask them, as I do on a regular basis, and you'll get some comments that align with what the teachers are saying above:

- I talk too much.
- I get distracted.
- I don't actively listen all lesson.
- I swing on my chair – I just need to move about!
- I lose focus.
- I argue back.
- I can be disrespectful.
- Boys get bored more easily and mess about more.
- Boys just want to be hard.
- Boys will always find something to make them laugh.

But you'll also get other comments that show much more clearly that there are many things that teachers and the school can be doing differently to help:

- Teachers talk too much.
- The lesson's not engaging.
- It's hard to concentrate for a long time – a double lesson without a break is a killer.
- Sometimes the work is too hard.
- I don't like it when:
  - You have to stop something you're halfway through.
  - We're repeating stuff we've done before.
  - It's a supply teacher you don't know.
  - You're copying from books or from the board.

- Boys wanna *do* stuff.
- I'm in bottom sets for everything, with my mates, and it's because of our behaviour. What chance is there?

Practical exercise

Why not try this exercise yourself, with a colleague, with your department or with your senior management team? You could even run it in a full-staff meeting. Avoid calling it: 'What's the matter with our boys?'!

Chapter 22
Be the change you'd like to see

> **Overview**
> - Remember how it felt for you
> - Making a difference
> - High expectations and why they're important

A parent approached me after one of my training sessions to tell me of his experience at secondary school. He was desperately unhappy throughout the entire five years. At a Year 9 parents' meeting, his parents were dragged from one disgruntled teacher to the next, to be given the very faintest of praise at each one. Then came the design technology teacher whose welcoming smile gave his mother the feeling that just maybe she could ask this one for help. After all, she'd garnered that her boy was keen on the subject from the extremely limited conversations she'd had with her son about his school day. She went straight to the heart of the matter and went with: 'Mr Martin, I wondered if you could help my boy. You see, he's doing so badly but he does love your subject. I wondered, is there anything, anything at all, you could do to make him love school just that little bit more?'

The teacher replied, in the kindest of tones, 'Of course, of course. How about, er (the teacher glanced down at the A3 sheet full of smaller-than-passport-sized photographs of his students), er, Paul, you pop along to me at lunchtime on Monday and we'll see what we can do about letting you do a design project at lunchtimes.'

A glimmer of hope lasted the long journey home, throughout the weekend and right up to Monday lunchtime, when it was cruelly and devastatingly extinguished. 'Yes lad?' bellowed the teacher at the sight of the poor lad standing in the doorway.

'Sir, you said at the parents' evening that I should come and see you… about a project, sir.'

The teacher looked at the boy, then looked one way, then the other way along the corridor outside his room and snarled, his eyes fixed firmly on the boy's, 'Why don't you just fuck off, son.'

'And that's what I did,' said the parent. 'It took me way into my 30s before I felt I could trust anyone again.'

This isn't the only such story I know. I've also heard:

- 'My son was told when he was ten that when he opened his mouth only rubbish came out. He's 30 and he's under therapy.'
- 'I'm pretty sure that every teacher in this school hates me.'
- 'One teacher called me a wimp the other week, a gob on legs, scum of the earth, a peasant and a parasite.'

Remember how it felt for you

In my own school days, a significant proportion of teachers were of working-class origin like myself, and we look back on a more divided and more brutal system. There are still thousands of teachers who are fired up because of the inequalities that exist in today's society, just like we were.

A friend and colleague of mine, who lived in a sprawling council estate in Leeds, passed his 11-plus, much to the pride of his parents. He had not been at the school for very long at all before there was a slight altercation with a member of staff, who in retaliation for what he considered to be barefaced cheek, called the boy a 'guttersnipe'. 'You're a guttersnipe,' said the teacher. At the time, my friend had no idea what that was, but because of the way it was said, he was clear that it wasn't a compliment. Upset, he told his dad, who didn't know the word either.

'You must have done something to upset him. Pass us here that [brand spanking new] school dictionary.' He handed his dad the dictionary from its pride of place on the mantlepiece and they read the definition together: 'Guttersnipe – a homeless vagabond, outcast boy or girl. A person of the lowest moral or economic station.' My friend told me that he and his mum had to virtually physically hold his dad back from charging up to 'that' school to 'leather' the teacher. 'To leather – to beat or thrash a person with a leather strap.' Of course, ironically, from that moment on, wild horses would not have dragged his father (or mother for that matter) into 'that' school.

It may well be that you or others around you suffered shortages, not just of soap and appropriate stationery, but also of bare necessities like food and warmth, love and understanding. Then remember how it made you feel, and bloody well make a difference.

High expectations

Been there, done that, got the T-shirt. But will you be wearing the T-shirt that says these words?

- 'What do you expect with this lot?'
- 'Oh no, not you lot again.'
- 'You're just as bad as your brother/sister/father/mother.'
- 'It's going to be locked horns, battle to the end.'
- 'I've got the classes I deserve.'

Or these?

- 'I'm here for you.'
- 'I believe in you.'
- 'I'm all ears.'
- 'I can't wait to tell you what we are doing this lesson.'
- 'Last lesson you did great. Wonder how you'll do with the next challenge.'

Having high expectations for boys is crucial in raising their achievement and aspirations. They do come out with the most amazing things sometimes. It may be in a discussion about *Macbeth* or a wonderful question in a P4C session. Well, if they've done it once, they can damned well do it again. It's like the story of the flea. You can try this at home if you've got fleas. You put a flea in a glass and it'll keep jumping, bless it. It'll jump higher than the glass then land in the glass again. If you put a piece of card across the top of the glass, the flea will keep on jumping, keep banging its little head time and time again, bless it. Then you take away the card and the flea will still keep jumping, but only as high as where you placed that card… It's wherever you set that level of expectation. (Apparently in research they discovered that the progeny of those fleas will never be able to jump higher either!) It reminds me too of a head of maths who told me he brought in one of his department at the end of the first half term to talk about the new Year 7s. He came straight to the point and said, 'Do you realise, your set 4 has done better than my set 2 in their end-of-half-term tests?'

The teacher looked puzzled. 'I wasn't teaching set 4. I was teaching set 2… er… wasn't I?' That blooming self-fulfilling prophecy, eh? If you're still thinking about those fleas, look up 'training fleas' on YouTube and there you will see a jam jar containing 200 fleas and, when they unscrew the lid, not a single flea flies out.

I hope by this point in the book that you are already very much on board with the changes that need to be made around boys' achievement. If you still need to convince some colleagues, however, why not try using this chapter to help?

Chapter 23
Street culture

> **Overview**
>
> - The influence of street culture in the 2020s
> - Drugs and boys
> - Social media and mental health
> - Knives and guns

When I first started working on raising boys' achievement, over 20 years ago, one of the barriers to boys' learning I would refer to was 'street culture'. At the time of writing my first book, in 2006, I exemplified street culture as offering boys protection, friendship, support, identity and a close-knit community. In short, many of the things that schools could and should be providing them with. In *Breaking Through Barriers to Boys' Achievement*, I said: 'Boys, particularly at the point of transition from primary school to high school, need all the help they can get in terms of developing an identity for themselves that sits comfortably not only with them, but also with their peers. If elements of their own culture are not valued then they look elsewhere to find that connection' (Wilson, 2013).

I referred predominantly to street culture in those days as being a rich tapestry of rap music, street art and break dance. I urged teachers to embrace elements such as street art in order to make that connection and subsequently add a new vibrancy to artwork created in school. I stand by the idea of making those connections but how times have changed. Street culture is a whole new ball game in the 2020s.

Drugs, guns and knife crime proliferate and schools have to play a significant role in educating, guiding and supporting perpetrators and victims. The things I advocated for schools providing back in 2006 – protection, friendship, support, identity and a close-knit community – have become increasingly more necessary and significantly more complex for schools to do with and they often need more help and advice from outside agencies. This is a key area to get to grips with as you work to pull together a plan for supporting your boys, so I'll go into a little more detail in this chapter.

Drug culture and boys

At the time of writing, there are a number of young men who are working within communities where drugs, alcohol and violent crime proliferate. One such person is Sam Tyrer, a registered nurse, who runs an organisation in Lancashire called Change Talks. The team delivers talks to young people in school about drugs, joining gangs, self-harm, suicide, the dangers of social media and more. Members of Change Talks have had first-hand experience of a variety of these issues, which makes the messages all the more potent.

With regard to drugs and boys (at the time of writing, cocaine, ketamine and cannabis are the three most popular drugs), they are often given free drugs by dealers, who are not much older than they are, for maybe a couple of weeks, and then told that they owe the dealers hundreds of pounds. Subsequently, as they can't put their hands on so much money, they have to deal for the dealers. Very often the dealers use Snapchat to bully and intimidate. 'If they refuse then very often their families are threatened by the dealers. At this point the pressures become too great for some and suicide provides the only way out.'

One member of the team also attempted suicide himself as a reaction towards the bullying he received as a teenager. Years later, having given up drink and drugs, he decided that, as a lucky survivor, he wanted to help young men who find themselves in circumstances such as his but who struggle to deal with the horror of their situations. When Sam and the team were conducting research into the issues, they discovered that Preston was the teenage suicide capital of the UK. One member of the team, having had issues himself, managed to turn himself around through phenomenal hard work and subsequently became totally determined to help these boys, many of whom had attempted suicide at the ages of 14 and 15.

Social media and mental health

At the time of writing, social media is playing a hugely significant role in creating mental health issues. Many more young men now hate their bodies as a result of programmes like *Love Island* and find themselves taking steroids and subsequently become more anxious and depressed. According to Sam, 'If they don't get an immediate response on a programme such as Snapchat, they get more and more anxious as they wait for a reaction. They know their message has been read (two blue ticks indicate that it has been read on WhatsApp, for example). The longer the wait after the blue ticks, the more anxious and lacking in self-confidence they become.'

So anxious are boys about the fact that nobody likes them that they are buying 'likes' and followers, hundreds at a time, to make themselves appear more popular and feel more confident. They become totally fixated by the number of followers they have and the number of followers their friends or peer leaders have.

There are even more chilling examples of the internet having a powerful, sickening influence. It is not uncommon, for example, to hear of youngsters posting videos of themselves self-harming. What is more, self-harm packs are available online to buy. As far as the issue of porn is concerned, children as young as five have watched pornography on the internet.

When you speak to some boys, they may surprise you by bringing up mental health as something that schools need to be doing more to help with. One boy told me, 'Mental health is disregarded. It needs to be more recognised that we go through a lot of stress daily. It's not just teachers.' The missing months of schooling due to COVID-19 in 2020, and the run-up to what turned out to be their non-existent exams at the end of Years 11 and 13, really brought emotional health and wellbeing issues to the fore as far as students were concerned. These issues will need to be front and centre for quite some time.

Knives and guns

According to the Home Office report, 'What works to prevent gang involvement, youth violence and crime' (O'Connor and Waddell, 2015), much of our knowledge on strategies that work in relation to knives and guns comes from the USA. That evidence shows that multi-agency, multi-focus strategies are more successful than single-focus interventions in combating gun violence among young people. The report states that programmes for children and young adolescents focus on problem solving, self-control, anger management, conflict resolution and socio-emotional skills. Evidence suggests they are particularly effective with at-risk children who are experiencing early-onset behavioural problems or who come from low-income backgrounds.

In the UK, it is clear that all schools would benefit from such programmes too. The 2010 Ofsted report, 'Safeguarding children and young people in education from knife crime', was a piece of research carried out in 29 schools, colleges and pupil referral units in London and included focus groups with parents and children. The research clearly showed that it was not down to a single agency, including schools, to solve knife crime. Instead the report recommended approaches by a variety of agencies working in cooperation, which are locally based and combine both prevention and suppression. The findings showed that these approaches are more effective than single interventions by agencies working in isolation.

Some schools in the Ofsted sample chose to use outside agencies to supplement the curriculum. This was done to great effect, as the outside agencies were seen to have greater credibility amongst young people and considered to possess better knowledge. In one setting where ex-gang members delivered sessions, staff said: 'It was amazing to watch. They could discuss music, had similar backgrounds, used the same language as our students. It was a shock to students to find out that after prison, ex-gang members struggled to get a mortgage, a bank account and couldn't travel to

America. They talked about when they were 16 and 17 and that it [joining a gang] seemed the coolest thing to do. It was a real eye opener for our students'.

Sharing experiences such as these can significantly enhance a well-developed PSHE programme. The common denominator among the vast majority of young boys (as it is indeed predominantly boys) involved in knife violence is their shared experiences of poverty and neglect. What is clear too is that 'street cred' and respect become, for some, the only ways in which they can feel valued. Acting to maintain their reputation and the 'respect' of others can provoke conflict and violence. It would surely be far better to make them feel valued, listened to, and afforded some respect in their school lives. When we focus on this, we really can and do make a difference.

Chapter 24
Pupil voice

> **Overview**
> - The right environment and atmosphere
> - Questions to try
> - Empower them: Big Ears Day and Changemakers

In this chapter, I hope to give you a clearer idea about how pupil voice projects can work in practice.

The right environment and atmosphere

It's October 2019 and in a fairly challenging UK secondary school, a group of ten (the optimum number I find is eight to ten) Years 10 and 11 boys arrive in the conference room for a whole hour of talking to some old bloke. I find that a setting like a conference room or interview room helps attribute an element of importance to the task ahead. Provide biscuits and juice as a small thank you and the stage is set. On this occasion, as is usually the case, it was a mixed group in terms of ability and self-confidence, the motivated and the not so, those able to readily express themselves and those who took until almost the end of the session before they really warmed to the idea of discussion. We had time for a full hour's discussion; no other adult was present. I have found that if any of their teachers are present, the change in quality of contributions, and saying it like it is, is rarely affected, unless that is, the teacher can't control themselves and joins in. It's important that the boys don't lose focus.

Of course, what very often happens is the boys I'll be having a discussion with are very suspicious about why they have been chosen. They'll often immediately establish a label for themselves as the troublemakers, the underachieving boys, the lazy oiks, whatever it is. Quite often, however, they have been prepared, told they are a representative group of all the boys in school who will be happy to join in with a group focusing on what the issues are around boys' achievement and what we and they can do about it. On occasion they're quite fired up when they arrive about the fact girls apparently do better than boys in everything at GCSE (apart from maths):

So, having established with them that I'm not an Ofsted inspector we're ready to start. So then, straight for the jugular: 'Why is it that girls tend to do better in school?' They're off and running, and pretty soon we have a checklist of all the things boys, by their own admission, need to do to improve their situation, and things that teachers need to address.

Questions to try

If your boys need a little more prompting, or you want to help guide the conversation, here are some questions to get you started.

- What makes a good teacher?
- What kind of teacher gets the best from you?
- How do you learn best?
- What excites you in lessons?
- What makes you want to learn?
- What are the things you'll never forget about school?
- What has been the single most useful thing a teacher has ever said to you?

Empower them

Projects involving pupil voice can range from the fun and engaging to the most transforming. They have one thing in common: they make those involved in the process feel empowered and that their points of view are worthy of consideration. Here are two examples of pupil voice projects at both ends of this spectrum.

Big Ears Day

All over one school I visited were A4 pictures of all their members of staff, each sporting huge Photoshopped ears and bearing the legend: 'BIG EARS DAY THIS FRIDAY.' Big Ears Day was held every half term on an appointed day. The formal school day finished 15 minutes early and, using every single adult in the building, what replaced it was a 20-minute discussion on topics of the day or pupils' individual concerns.

In groups of approximately one adult to seven or eight pupils, the subjects for discussion included the reward system; the school day; uniform; setting; behaviour; discipline; homework; lunchtime; the library and peer pressure.

It was made abundantly clear that this was not the opportunity for a moan but, if there were things that needed attention, they would all emerge from their sessions with practical solutions that might be explored. And these might be explored further when six outstanding contributors (chosen by members of small discussion groups) joined the head and senior managers for lunch at the 'captain's table'.

Changemakers

On a much more ambitious scale, Penryn College developed a transformative pupil voice project called 'The Changemakers'.

The Changemakers: Penryn College

Penryn College began a project in January 2014 to help turn around boys in danger of underachieving. They decided there was only one place to start and that was with the boys themselves. Their plan was to:

1. listen to the observations of their newest, high-achieving Year 7 boys
2. commission a group of identified Year 9 boys to investigate boys' learning
3. get boys to report back to the wider school community
4. endow them with the power to make changes to further the expectations for all boys in the school.

Interviews with the Year 7 boys gave the school an insight into the keys to success. The common responses were:

- parental support
- clear preparation for KS2 SATs and a knowledge of what SATs meant for them
- a love of new challenges
- a thirst for new knowledge.

The barriers to success appeared to include:

- Some groups felt disruptive students were taking up valuable learning time.
- Some students didn't know what they needed to do in order to get to the next level in all subjects.

Immediately after these discussions, a staff working group was formed to share thoughts on boys from research and college data. Staff feedback focused initially on the need to increase boys' engagement and to inject an ethos of success and a belief that 'success matters'. Feedback also covered the need for instant feedback and appropriate rewards, for parity between boys and girls at rewards evenings and for basic social skills to be addressed consistently.

The next phase was to meet with Year 9 boys as an entire year group and highlight the issues that staff believed were currently negatively affecting boys' achievement, such as low aspirations and limited self-belief. This culminated in 45 boys signing up for the project. The college followed this with a parents' evening to share information about the project's positive intentions and about how parents could help. The meeting was very well attended.

Through subsequent discussions with their peers, boys provided staff with useful feedback about how boys seemed to learn best, as well as the circumstances in which boys learned less well. At the end of the 2014 academic year, the group had 'Learning Leaders' training on good learning skills. This created really worthwhile dialogue. At this point it was decided that the groups of boys would be called the 'Changemakers' to recognise their contributions and their potential to affect change.

Autumn 2014

At the beginning of their Year 10, following a meeting with the head, the boys set about exploring the following question with their peers: 'What do we expect Key Stage 4 boys to be like in terms of being:

1. highly skilled
2. keen to learn
3. well qualified
4. socially adjusted?'

These became known as the 'Big 4' and this formed the framework of their subsequent action plan. In groups, the boys led discussions into what each of the 'Big 4' meant for them. Then came the biggest task: leading a whole-staff meeting. The students shared their findings with over 80 staff members. The boys then led 12 small discussion groups to ascertain the staff's criteria for the 'Big 4' and to do a strengths, weaknesses, opportunities and threats (SWOT) analysis. The boys presented themselves well in the meeting, drawing out a range of opinions from staff in an open and honest way. Staff feedback was positive and they valued the opportunity to talk to pupils. One teacher fed back, 'I really valued the honesty of the pupils' and a pupil said, 'It was good being able to talk to the teachers about our learning like that.'

Next steps for the Changemakers

The Changemakers carried out similar tasks with pupils in tutor time, with parents at the parents' forum, at a governors' meeting and also with the primary partnership. They then created an action plan based on the 'Big 4' by gathering all consultation documents and identifying commonalities. They had to decide how to make this document relevant, to be used by pupils, staff and parents, as well as developing monitoring arrangements.

The Changemakers successfully led a second staff meeting to put the outlines of their plan to their teachers. The aim was to ensure that students and staff were all focused on what had been mutually agreed as the 'Big 4':

1. Being keen to learn.
   Being enthusiastic and motivated; having aspirations; being happy to take on responsibility; being organised and punctual; completing coursework and homework.

2. Being highly skilled.
   Communicating, problem-solving, being creative and original; being able to reflect on learning.

3. Being well-qualified.
   Being on trajectory for every subject area (in this case, being on course for five A* – C grades); being confident in literacy and numeracy.

4. Being socially adjusted.
   Being respectful; having good manners; working well in a team; being confident in communication; taking part beyond academic work.

Spring 2015

In January, the Changemakers met and had training from Gary Wilson. The students had a series of talks about attitudes to learning, healthy lifestyles and aspirations.

In February, it was decided that the lower down the school this began, the more valuable the result would be. Subsequently, Year 8 and 9 students had a learning consultation event on 'the Year 8 curriculum and becoming a Changemaker', led by the Year 10 Changemakers. The Year 10 Changemakers were widely felt to be real positive role models when working with younger students. As a result, at this point, there were now 32 potential Changemakers from the lower school who were keen to be involved!

Feedback from Gary Wilson: Your work is virtually unique in the country and as such you should be very proud of the changes you are making for generations of boys to come. It was an absolute pleasure to spend time with you and may I wish you all great success. With best wishes, Gary.

In March, the Changemakers met with education advisers from Cornwall Council, who were keen to support their action plan. They recommended the boys write to them with the areas where they would like support.

Summer 2015

In June, the Year 10 Changemakers were invited to be a case study for Cornwall Council's 'Raising Aspiration and Achievements Strategy', which included presenting a report on their work to other schools. The Changemakers were also invited to the local head teachers' meeting to present their work.

Following the success of Gary Wilson's student training and subsequent advertising for new lower school recruits, the 32 Year 8 Changemakers:

- met with the Year 10 Changemakers
- carried out team-building activities to develop the identity of the group
- had discussions around what leadership looks like
- began a review of their learning.

Meanwhile, the Year 10 Changemakers diligently worked away at monitoring and developing their action plans. There were now four lead students working on the 'Big 4' areas, who met with SLT links to help make their action plan a reality. For example, one group met with senior staff about the homework system, while another group met about the report system. The Changemakers were also keen to see boys' learning in action. As such, they had training from lead practitioners in carrying out learning walks, observing a group of key Year 8 students to see if their learning matched the Changemakers' expectations. The learning walks allowed the boys to identify further areas for development in September 2015.

In June, staff were updated on 'priorities for boys' learning' in a briefing meeting. This was done as part of getting ready for September 2015. The priorities were:

1. *A discussion about setting in the lower school*
2. *Changemaker learning walks*
3. *Best practice reported back*
4. *Confirm teaching and learning issues for continuous professional development*

5. *Heads of Department/House create a 'year's learning journey' to be displayed*
6. *Action plan meeting with SLT and Changemaker links*
7. *Year 8 Changemakers established set programme of work for September*
8. *Data monitoring of the progress of Changemakers*
9. *All tutor groups to have a representative*
10. *Changemakers' journey for the year mapped out*

The results

After 18 months, the school had:

- an overt approach to narrowing the gender gap
- a whole-school action plan for boys' learning following full consultation
- a new reporting system to monitor and measure the impact on achievement
- a reporting system that went beyond academic attainment and effort, to consider social skills and boys' wider development
- student observers as learning leaders
- 'spotlight' students established for targeting GCSE boys' intervention tutor group
- a new language with which to engage in meaningful dialogue about the 'Big 4' with students, staff, parents and other stakeholders around boys' learning
- a new shared understanding developed through student voice and stakeholder consultation, as exemplified in the 'Boys' Audit' tool below, designed to be used in pupil mentoring.

Boys' Audit: having the right information

The following is an example of a piece of research carried out at Penryn College.

Complete an audit based on teachers' 'instinct' of the student from performance in their subject using a four point scale (this takes around 30 seconds per student). This can be used as a mentoring discussion in tutor time and as a planning tool for staff to maximise personalisation of boys' learning.

Apply a number to each area:

1	Exceptional: exceeds expectation and goes above and beyond.
2	Good: is an acceptable level and is effective.
3	Requires improvement: could be improved with focus from student or support.
4	Cause of concern: an area of concern that will impact student progress.

An example of a Year 11 student's audit in one subject area:

Keen to learn	2.8	Highly skilled	3	Socially adjusted	3.6
Enthusiastic	3	Communicates	3	Respectful	1
Motivated	3	Solves problems	3	Well mannered	1
Has aspirations	3	Creative and original	3	Works well in a team	2
Takes on responsibility	3	Reflects on learning	3	Confident communicator	3
Organised	3	Takes risks/resilient	2	Leadership	3
Punctual	2			Takes part beyond academic work	3
Completes coursework	2				
Completes homework	3				

Impacts

On entry, boys have a point score which is on average a third lower than girls.

Year	Gender gap	5A* CEM %	Basics %	English LoP v A-C		Maths		Valued Added	Progress 8
2014	Girls	75	75	72		73	79	1002	n/a
	Boys	52	52	57		61	71	977	n/a
	Gap	23	23	15	27	12	8	25	n/a
2015	Girls	68	68	83	79	76	79	1035	0.47
	Boys	42	46	65	53	66	71	1014	0.21
	Gap	26	22	18	26	10	8	21	0.26
2016	Girls	67	70	92	89	75	72	1042	0.56
	Boys	63	70	85	78	75	73	1015	0.19
	Gap	4	0	7	11	0	-1	27	0.37

© *Penryn College 2017*

Two years later: we made a difference!

What, according to the staff, helped to make the difference?

- Boys considered 'cultural architects' in the Changemakers project.
- Targeting key students at a whole school, department and teacher level.
- Relentless exam practice and feedback.
- High expectations and positive relationships.
- A strong emphasis on a range of revision strategies.

Some key messages for staff arising out of dialogue with Changemakers from Years 7 to Year 10:

- Insist on high expectations for all.
- Vary tasks to keep us focused.
- Warnings and consequences need to be consistently applied.
- Seat individuals carefully, including with mixed-gender seating.
- Have consistent routines, for example, set homework at the start of lessons.
- Engage boys in specific roles and responsibilities.
- Develop student leaders.
- Provide a clear topic overview and then set short-term targets.
- Share data with us so we can see our progress.
- Make the long-term learning journey clear.

One boy said the following about the Changemaker project: 'It means I am more confident talking in front of people. I've had some hard questions. This made us more articulate and better at coping under pressure.' Another said, 'It was good being able to talk to the teachers about our learning in a different way. They have valued our honesty. We have valued theirs.'

Things can happen when you listen

With one group of Year 11s, I was talking about positivity and just how powerful it can be, and a head of year sat in on the discussion: 'I'm thinking hard now about my mood when a new class arrives. Up to today, if I've had Year 8 first thing, God help the next class and they know it's not right. They've made me realise it's not right too! I've gone into my Year 10 class today that I normally have problems with and I told them that they'd been really good the last two lessons and I said, "So let's have another!" and we did!' Another boy in the same discussion declared, 'I hate it when a teacher takes their last lesson into yours – you can always tell.' Another valuable chunk of information for us to deal with as we may.

Act

It's common and sometimes necessary for teachers to create a fuss with a class or an individual when a boundary has been overstepped but less common for some teachers to compliment them when things are going sweetly. What can you compliment *those boys* on today? Maybe: 'It was great the way all of you focused on the poem today. Thank you.'

Student Subject Learning Review

	Department/Subject
	Year group
This survey is an opportunity to say what you have enjoyed about your learning and what could have been better.	**Agree** ⟶ **Disagree**
1. I have enjoyed this topic/project	
a. I have understood the work	
b. I have been encouraged to do my best	
c. The work was at the right level so that I increased my knowledge and skills	
d. I have received regular feedback	
e. The feedback has helped me improve my work	
f. I have received regular homework	
g. The homework was at the right level for me	
h. I have received written feedback on my homework	
2. I have experienced different ways of learning	
a. Talking and discussion	
b. Audio-visual material on the whiteboard	
c. I have been encouraged to discuss my work with others.	
d. I have been able to work in a group	
e. I have been encouraged to ask questions	
f. I have been able to use ICT	
3. I have received regular praise and encouragement	
a. My teacher knows if I have understood the work	
b. I know what level/grade I am working at	

4. What do you think you did well in this unit of work or project?

5. What did you enjoy about this unit of work or project?

6. This project or unit of work would have been better if…

Chapter 25
Turning things around

> **Overview**
> - 'Please can you tell teachers to talk about the good things we do?'
> - Is it ever too late?
> - 'How about if I say to all your teachers that you'd like to turn yourself around?'
> - Advice to Year 7s from Year 11s: 'I wish I'd been a nerd.'

Before and after group discussions, usually with around ten boys selected by the school, I will say to the boys that I will be passing on their thoughts on school, their opinions and their concerns to staff. Usually this will be during a twilight session for staff and sometimes to parents at a parents' session immediately after the twilight. Sometimes they pay it little attention but sometimes the penny drops and they become aware of the power of the situation and grasp the opportunity to pass on messages.

> **What I'd like to see**
>
> 'If you are going to talk to teachers about us, can you ask them to remember and talk to us about the good things we've done and not just the bad, because that just kind of knocks you a bit… it feels like a spiral.'

One Year 9 boy told me a familiar story: 'I've actively tried to start paying more attention in lessons, actively changed my personality… changing the way I act.'
'Has it been picked up?'
A shake of the head.
'What a shame, I guess that must be disappointing?'
A nod.

His classmate said, 'I've had that before – I've told teachers I really do want to work hard – then I've tried… they kind of take that on board, but as soon as you do anything slightly wrong, they'll use that to get at you and sometimes say something sarcastic, in front of your mates like, "So here we go again then…"'

Another added, 'I've tried saying it to a teacher but I can't control my tongue and I just make it worse.' And another told me he really wants a fresh start, but he's convinced there's no point trying.

Another echoed his experience exactly, 'Yeah, I've had that before. I really do want to try, then I'll have a bad lesson or something… then it goes back to where I was.'

His friends concurred, 'I decided to work hard and sort myself out but I still got called out. I tried for a while and nobody noticed, so I thought why bother?'

'You can be good for a whole term then one slip and you're back down a grade.'

'I don't know how to get from a three to a one – you're told to go to teachers for feedback, but I don't feel that I can sometimes.'

'You can't really do that… go and say anything, unless you've got a decent relationship with a teacher.'

One added, woefully, 'The next time I see a teacher after a bad lesson I go in thinking, here we go again, and I'm just kind of waiting to be shouted at.'

And on and on, a litany of gloom and doom.

It's never too late

If you're going to be starting a project to make things better for boys, it's time for all staff to acknowledge that boys can turn things around. Boys need to be given a clean slate and they need to be praised for their efforts to move forward. It's never too late, even for boys in Years 10 and 11.

'It's too late to change it' is something I hear a lot in group discussions with Years 10 and 11. 'No, it's not,' I say all the time. 'It's never too late.' I've lost count of the number of times a Year 10 or 11 boy has said to me, 'I wish I'd been a swot/nerd/geek/wimp/keeno/teacher's pet/square/squarebear/sweat/spoff/boff/boffin/stew/sook' or 'I want to do well. I wish I'd not just fallen in with my mates and wasted all that time.' They are very clear about what can really help bring about change. Sometimes the answers are about the small stuff that makes a big difference, for example, 'When I've been told the positives' or 'When I've had some praise, when I've been told in a lesson that I'm doing well, that changes everything.'

❝❝ What I'd like to see

'When I feel like I'm doing well in a subject and I get told I'm working well, that makes a lot of difference. It even changes the way I walk into the next

> lesson. I'm thinking, right, I'm doing well – I want to carry on doing well. If I'm told I'm not doing well, I've got no motivation to work harder. It's the way I am.'

One Year 10 boy spoke to me about the power of sorry when it comes to change. He shared: 'I think maybe I need to give some teachers a second chance too! There are some teachers that I can talk to about why things have happened and then I never do anything wrong again for that teacher because from then on we get on really well. Sometimes I think saying sorry and meaning it is the only thing to do.'

After a group discussion with ten bright Year 11s, a teacher who had sat in with the discussion said to me that the majority of staff were just waiting for certain boys from that group to leave, and that the staff were just counting down the days and that she felt that was very sad. I agreed. The group had a very low opinion of themselves, of their school and of their teachers. I said to them, 'If I give your teachers this list of names, your names, and told them, "These boys are serious, they want to turn themselves around," what would you think about that?'

Silence.

'Yes!' said one.

'It's not easily done though,' said another.

'You'd only have to do the slightest thing wrong and they'd still get at you, with "I see you're back in your old ways again…"' added the first.

'Yeah, a few days later they'd throw it back in your face and say, "I thought you'd said you wanted to…"' agreed the first.

'So, do you want me to try?' I said.

A few nodded. So I did.

Act

Do it! In a staff meeting, invite members of staff to comment on the positive – and only the positive – aspects of 'those boys'. 'He works OK for me' might or might not be a great opener – you know your staff best!

Ask Year 11s to give advice to Year 7s

'I wish I could go back to Year 7. I would have thought about myself instead of everyone else. I wouldn't have messed about at all. I wouldn't have shown off as much. I would've knuckled down. I'd have been a boff. I could have been one but I turned it down. I wanted to be one of the lads.'

I ask Year 11s regularly what advice they would give to Year 7s to help them achieve more. This advice for Year 7s, from a small group of struggling Year 11 boys, is typical of the responses I get for this question. They, like so many hundreds of boys I've spoken to, clearly know what they could and should have done. If only there had been some Year 11s around who might have passed on this advice to them!

If you want to do well:

- ✓ 'Work hard.'
- ✓ 'Be nice – no excuses.'
- ✓ 'At least make an attempt at homework – at least try. Your teacher won't mind so long as you've tried.'
- ✓ 'Don't get too distracted.'
- ✓ 'Get organised.'
- ✓ 'Give and take with teachers.'
- ✓ 'Get your head down.'
- ✓ 'Work to your highest standard.'
- ✓ 'Revise!!'
- ✓ 'Improve your attitudes with teachers.'
- ✓ 'Do it for yourself.'
- ✓ 'Respect teachers more.'
- ✓ 'Respect yourself.'
- ✓ 'Improve your behaviour.'
- ✓ 'Don't let anyone else drag you down.'
- ✓ 'Hang around with people with positive attitudes.'

Act

Have a discussion with a group of Year 11 boys on the subject of giving advice to Year 7s. You may want to bite the bullet and get the Year 11s to address Year 7s directly in a discussion.

Chapter 26

Mentoring boys: the Breakthrough way

> **Overview**
>
> - The National Education Breakthrough Programme: mentoring groups of boys
> - The interviews
> - Engaging parents
> - Boys' ideas of the mentoring process
> - Label free
> - The good news noticeboard
> - In a form group of their own

From 2008 until 2013, I was chair of The National Education Breakthrough Programme for raising boys' achievement (see Figure 26.1 on page 168). We worked with 30 different secondary schools a year, and every school had a small team focusing on a boys' project. Boys' opinions of the project were universally positive. A part of the project that was common across all schools was the mentoring of groups of boys, usually around a dozen and mostly in Year 8, following the model I had applied in my own school.

> **Think**
>
> Do you have mentoring of any kind in your school? Does it work well? Or does it fail to make a difference as overstreched SLTs struggle sometimes to make it to regular appointments? If it's the latter, have you tried or, if not, have you considered, group mentoring?

Figure 26.1 The poster campaign for The National Education Breakthrough Programme.

> **Act**
>
> Try following the mentoring process that follows in your own school.

The mentoring process

The process involved interviews with all the boys to ascertain whether or not:

1. They would be suited to join the team on the Breakthrough Programme.
2. They were keen to raise their own aspirations.
3. They were keen to turn themselves around.

Once the selection was made, the first event in most schools was to have an evening when parents were invited to hear all about the positive benefits of being on the Breakthrough Programme. In the majority of schools, the boys were involved in planning the event, from creating invitations to preparing and serving supper. The boys loved this: 'Me mum couldn't believe that they'd trusted me to do some cooking', 'I felt right proud of myself.'

> **Act**
>
> Plan and deliver an introductory evening (with or without – although preferably with – food prepared by the boys). Involve staff, parents and boys in the process, by sharing expectations and a commitment to make a difference. Outline the plan for the year, including, for example, plans to work on leadership skills, monitoring behaviour and subject grades, motivation scores, and so on.

One school revealed that, much to their amazement, whilst interviewing the boys for their place in their mentoring team, more or less every single boy expressed the same three hopes and desires. Each one wanted a mentor who would:

- 'get teachers to stop shouting at me'
- 'get teachers to give me help when I need it'
- 'get teachers to give me another chance when I need it'.

None had been prompted. It's a tough call going to a teacher as a 14-year-old and saying, 'I realise I've been a pain but I really want to turn things around and do well.

Could you give me another chance?' That's not to mention the legions of boys who have told me, as we saw on page 163, 'I tried to make a fresh start' or 'I started to behave better at the end of Year 9 but nobody noticed.' When I heard this, whimsical as it might sound, I had a thousand pin badges made that said 'LABEL FREE', meaning drop the label, or 'I'm fighting to change my label. Give me another chance.' And when I visited the groups in school, I would ask them, 'If I was to tell your teachers, if you see a badge, this is what it means, would you wear it?' A resounding 'yes!' wherever I went. 'If you abuse it you will lose it…?' Still a resounding yes! As a small part of an overwhelmingly powerful project to turn boys around, this was a very useful tool.

Act

Consider producing badges for your mentees (and anyone else desiring a turnaround, maybe).

Each school's group of boys, around ten to a dozen, were mentored on a twice-weekly basis. Quite a number of schools decided to put the whole group together as a form group. Regardless of whether they chose this approach, the groups, from a grand total of 150 secondary schools, almost invariably began to develop a positive identity from the outset. What's more, parental involvement had never been as good in almost every single school in the project. Parents, previously frustrated about their boys, finally felt that their cries for help had been listened to and that their boys were being given the help and understanding that they firmly believed they needed.

The schools chose a name for their groups. They were called Top Lads, High Five, No Limits, Breakthrough Boys, and so on. The staff team created displays within the staff room to celebrate the way in which these boys were actively working to turn themselves around. Some displays contained copies of praise emails that staff had sent to the boys (see Figure 26.2 on page 171). The boys would love those.

Extremely popular too were what came to be called the good news noticeboards. I suggested that all project schools should create a noticeboard (which became known later as the good news noticeboard) where they should display photographs of each of the boys in their mentoring group (this works in other contexts with groups of boys the school is concerned about) and where all adults in the building were instructed to place a positive sticky note next to the picture of the boy who'd been kind or helpful, polite or hardworking – in other words, anything positive.

Mentoring boys: the Breakthrough way

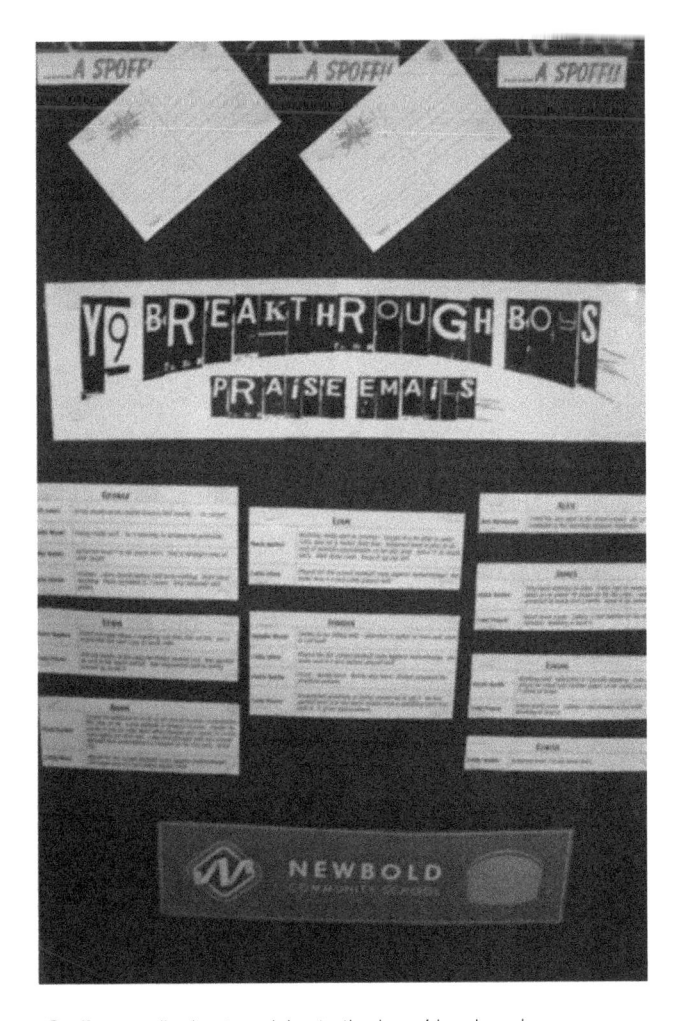

Figure 26.2 Staff room display to celebrate the boys' hard work.

When the first boy got a piece of good news from the good news noticeboard then suddenly everybody became desperate for good news. It changed a lot of boys' attitudes towards themselves. It changed a lot of teachers' attitudes towards the boys and, significantly, it changed the attitude of teachers who had never even taught the boys, just heard them complained about in the staff room – something we do, although we know damned well we shouldn't.

I asked one boy about what he thought about the good news noticeboard and he said, 'You know what's best? It's that we always knew that teachers talk about you and bitch about you in the staff room. Now they're still talking about you but in a good sort of way. I don't mind that!'

I can say in all honesty that within the context of the project's 150 schools, the thing that made the most difference, the thing that turned things around, was the fact that all those groups of boys were being given that extra little bit of genuine human interest in them as people. A little bit of love can go a long way.

In a significant number of the Breakthrough schools, the groups of boys were in a form that was exclusively theirs. 'I love it,' said one, midway through the project. 'You start every day really positive with different tips and advice and stuff.' Another said, 'It's like we have our own coach first thing in the morning.' Yet another, 'It's great. Sir makes us hot chocolate and toast in the morning.' The benefits were many:

- The form tutor or mentor could start off every day with positive words of encouragement. (More than a few teachers involved in this typical Breakthrough project strategy firmly believed that intensive mentoring of this sort helped to shift an entire cohort.)
- When things had gone wrong for one of the mentees the day before, strategies could be discussed between the group to get things right.
- Top tips for improving their work and behaviour were a regular feature of tutorial time.
- Successes for individual members of the group could be celebrated together.
- The group developed a positive identity that made them intent on making a difference for all.

One teacher involved suggested, 'They did have a strong identity before, but of a different kind. These boys started off with high self-esteem, but not as learners. With daily interventions and lots of positive feedback two or three times a day, that changed massively.' One boy, describing his experience in one such group told me, 'I couldn't believe the teacher was giving up all this time to get things right for us.' Another added, 'I liked it when sir said at the beginning of the year, "I'm going to be sticking my neck out for you.".' One mentor described the process as 'a way of keeping up, not catching up, by giving them love and support and real practical help.' And one boy, showing how much he valued the project simply said, 'Why can't the whole school be like this?'

As a mentor or as a form teacher or anyone involved in pastoral work, you might like to try the self-scoring motivation score sheet on the following page. It was devised for the National Education Breakthrough Programme and used extensively. Some schools even produced a parental version so that parents could communicate with school if there were to be serious dips to deal with or pleasing movements to show appreciation of.

Motivation: Pupil self-assessment guide

As used by the National Education Breakthrough Programme

9	My motivation is excellent. I am always cooperative with the teacher. I am enthusiastic and hardworking. I always do my best in my schoolwork. I am self-disciplined.
8	My motivation is between good and excellent.
7	My motivation is good. I am usually enthusiastic and hardworking. I try my best in my schoolwork or homework without requiring undue pressure.
6	My motivation is between satisfactory and good.
5	My motivation is satisfactory. I am usually cooperative with the teacher, but generally I do little more than is required by my teacher in terms of my schoolwork or homework.
4	My motivation is between poor and satisfactory.
3	My motivation is poor. I need constant pressure and attention from the teacher to ensure that I do some work. I do not do homework unless I'm pressured into it.
2	Motivation is between poor and very poor.
1	My motivation is very poor. I am uncooperative with and indifferent towards my teacher and my learning for most of the time in class. I make very little effort in my schoolwork or my homework. I lack self-discipline.

Act

Trial the idea of putting your mentees in the same form for half a term. Make the commitment at the outset that you will extend half term by half term if it works well, shifts any negative attitudes and raises levels of motivation.

Chapter 27

Raising boys' achievement in an inner London school: a case study

> **Overview**
> - A case study from an inner London school:
>   - The context
>   - What we did
>   - The report
>   - The results

To conclude, I'd like to present a case study of a school I worked with to help raise boys' achievement. Within a secondary school of over 1,200 pupils, it was agreed as part of my involvement with the school as a consultant that I would lead group discussions with the pupils to learn more about what the school could do to improve things for boys. Based on these pupil voice exercises, we came up with a report to all staff explaining the issues that were uncovered and recommendations from me for their next steps. You will see the report in full below. I hope this will show you what can be achieved and inspire you to run a similar project in your own school.

The context

The school was a large, inner-city secondary school with a significant gap between boys and girls at Key Stages 3 and 4. There was a committed staff team ready to listen to colleagues and boys about their individual experiences in order to help reduce the gap.

What we did

We conducted group interviews with a selection of boys. The groups were carefully selected to represent a range of different abilities, but we kept the groups at no more than ten to a dozen in number. After the interviews, we gave feedback to staff as part of a training session that I led. We then established a working group of staff to focus on a specific boys project. Some of the feedback was also shared in a parents' session that I ran.

The report

A report back to staff from Key Stages 3 and 4 student discussion groups with recommendations from Gary Wilson (GW).

With regard to teaching and learning, it was felt that sometimes teachers can race through content, delivering 'machine gun lessons'.

- GW: This can be challenging for boys as they require reflection time and good assessment for learning practice. It is well understood that the weakest link in the learning process for many boys is their inability to reflect. Many just want to get on with the next thing. 'Trying to learn without reflection is like trying to fill the bath without putting the plug in.'

Boys seem to be reticent to plan, which needs to be addressed.

- GW: Systematic approaches, particularly where this includes graphic organisers (mindmaps, etc.), are needed. (For a comprehensive collection of graphic organisers, see *Think it – Map it!* by Oliver Caviglioli.)

The rewards system needs to be improved.

- GW: Boys were critical of the school's current reward system, which they felt was inconsistent. 'We get plenty when we are in Year 7 and Year 8, but teachers seem to think that after that we're not interested.' Reward systems fail most significantly where peer pressure has got a tighter grip. Consultations with pupils will clearly help to create the most effective reward systems. Praise postcards and phone calls or text messages home are always surefire winners for boys.

We need to work on boys and reading.

- GW: Talking with the boys about their involvement in reading, many (around 60 to 70 per cent) said that they were rarely or even never read to as children. What's more, it would largely be mums doing the reading. Also, as appears to be the norm, the vast majority said that they never saw a man around the house reading, and if they did they only saw us reading the newspaper or an instruction booklet. It's no wonder a lot of boys come into primary schools thinking that reading is a girly thing to do. Discussing with all groups of boys reading for pleasure, many boys said they did it before they came to the high school, but now there were more 'important' and 'enjoyable' things to do with their time. Students have a free reading session once a week. The English department is now promoting more fiction for boys. There is also an idea to encourage male teachers from different subjects to attend the beginning of the reading sessions and talk about their favourite books. The national picture is that around 80 per cent of boys in secondary schools do not read at all for pleasure. School libraries are often full of boys at lunchtime, but they're not reading; they're just seeking sanctuary (from what we used to call the 'killing ground' in the sixties). Consider presenting reading as a challenge – a Year 7 reading challenge, Year 8 reading challenge, and so on, can help. Or how about an 'extreme reading challenge' (with pupils reading in unusual locations)? A real visual presence (posters of significant boys in school or male PE teachers and so on reading) can also help. Suspending the timetable for an hour every day for a week, six times a year, and encouraging the whole school to read fiction can really get boys reading regularly. 'Yes, I read now… Why? Because I have to!'

Boys in the school are influenced by street culture and anti-social behaviour.

- GW: Street culture is akin to another business that has opened up down the street and it is stealing our customers! Why? Because it offers them a sense of excitement, a sense of belonging, and even a sense of safety. But surely, isn't that what we should be doing? We have two choices: we embrace some of the positive elements – street art or music – and use them to make a connection, or we reject all elements out of hand and commit more boys to the street. But of course what is often regarded as street culture now involves more than grafitti, music and dance. Dealing with the sometimes deadly elements of drug-related knife and gun crime requires expert handling in school with an authentic voice that has real credibility.

NEWSFLASH: Many boys see science as 'boring' as they spend most of the time copying from books. The boys really enjoy the experiments and practical work but it doesn't happen enough as far as they are concerned.

- GW: According to a teacher's union survey of a few years ago, on average, 60 per cent of writing in high schools is copied from books or from boards. A rough audit of all the groups of boys spoken to today suggest that the figure is slightly higher than that. When asked 'in how many of your five lessons yesterday did you copy out a chunk of writing from books or from the board?' the range was between three and four boys in each group.

On the subject of after-school detentions, they resented them as they felt they were pointless. Furthermore, they felt that they weren't a powerful incentive to make them work or change their behaviour.

- GW: A review of a punishment system which 'attracts' the same boys week after week is clearly failing to do the job. As with rewards, pupil voice can be helpful here too. One boy suggested that losing their own leisure time at lunchtime might be more effective.

Boys found homework challenging, as there was much more than they were getting at primary schools. 'Why do we have to do homework? We do enough work at school!' was a view strongly shared by the rest of the groups.

- GW: Check on 'motivation rankings' around homework. This is a self-assessment grid for pupils to rank their motivation levels. It was developed by the National Breakthrough Programme and can be seen on page 173.

According to many boys in the groups, teachers spend too much time explaining concepts and ideas in lessons. Boys preferred interactive lessons and group work which helped them to think. Boys say they like to figure things out.

- GW: Boys always say we talk too much! We do need to pay attention to the fact that boys tend to need a challenge to spur them on. Problem-solving is seen as more engaging, as are more hands-on opportunities.

Boys in our school tend to favour teachers in subjects like drama and art as they feel that they are listened to more in these subjects and that the atmosphere in those classrooms is more laid back. All of the boys in all groups said they loved our discussion but it was something they informed me they hardly ever did.

- GW: You do sometimes hear yourself as a teacher say, don't you, 'That was a brilliant discussion but we'd better pick up our pens and get on with some work' – completely dismissing the value of a discussion. As boys' writing was such a cause for concern, it would be really useful if more discussion as well as debate and role play could take place generally but particularly as a precursor to writing.

Boys disliked sarcasm that teachers sometimes used at a boy's expense in the classroom. When talking with a group of staff on one occasion about how we talk to boys, one teacher enthusiastically proffered, 'Sarcasm, I use sarcasm with boys. They love sarcasm.' What?! Belittling a boy in front of his mates is a pretty surefire way of ending that relationship.

- GW: Boys are not only the best barometers of good teaching but also the best barometers of good teachers. They will not respond positively to teachers who do not show them respect but expect to receive it themselves.

Some boys said that there isn't enough creative writing in English; it was almost always just answering questions.

- GW: Surprisingly to some, creative writing is almost invariably the kind of writing that boys like in primary schools. This element needs to be nurtured more and not just in English lessons. Getting creative in history or science can pay huge dividends. (One science teacher told me that the very best work he had received in years was when he informed the class that they were going to explore pondlife, but in a slightly different way. They were first introduced to pondlife in a fairly traditional way, learning about the variety of species that could be found, their appearance, eating habits, etc. Then he told them that what he was looking for was an adventure story from them, working in pairs, imagining themselves to be in a minute submarine journeying around the pond, detailing their encounters with the creatures inhabiting the pond. 'The water louse lashed out with its mighty claws, pulverising the flank of the submarine in one devastating swing. The sickening screech of grinding metal was followed by the submarine plunging into the deep, dark abyss.' He was amazed at the results. I asked what inspired this idea. 'Einstein!' he said. 'It's how he worked out the theory of relativity. He imagined himself as a beam of light!'

Boys felt that long-term targets and 'blanket' targets like 'improve your handwriting' were not welcome. They want to know how to improve their work.

- GW: Assessment for learning could have been written with just boys in mind, as we have seen elsewhere. The structural approach, the use of success criteria and short-term targets work best for boys.

There was lots of negativity expressed about pupil grouping from Year 7, such as 'I'm in bottom set because of my behaviour and the work in lower sets is too easy.' One boy said, 'There are a lot of clever people in lower sets because of target grades – they use the grades from primary school and I didn't really care in primary. I thought high school was where all the serious stuff happened.'

The results

All students were made aware of their colleagues' findings via school council meetings. Staff were made aware of the outcomes of the discussions with boys via a staff meeting and whole-school twilight session. The outcomes were as follows:

- A pupil forum was established as a way of continuing the extremely useful feedback from our discussions.
- Staff considered a range of issues and suggestions from the boys in faculties.
- Staff acted upon modifying the nature of lessons along the lines that boys had suggested, for example the need for more reflection time, with a review of plenaries as a faculty and the trial of new ones (as PDSAs; see page 115).
- The heads of faculty reviewed the reward system and invited the school council to engage in action research into pupils' feelings about rewards and sanctions and report back to staff.
- The issue of boys' attitudes towards and engagement with reading was explored through heads of faculty meetings. They agreed to half-termly 'drop everything and read days'. They also agreed to creating book displays in faculties of fiction and non-fiction related to their subjects.
- The school librarian introduced reading challenges for Years 7 and 8, which successfully increased the amount of fiction boys were reading.
- As writing was highlighted by almost all the boys involved in the discussions, this became a significant faculty agenda item, for example, by monitoring the amount of copying from the board, being more understanding about boys' handwriting and helping boys structure their writing through the use of graphics.
- Pupil grouping also became an ongoing agenda item with staff.

References

Biddulph, S. (2018), *Raising Boys in the 21st Century*. London: Thorsons.
Book Trust (2020), 'More than a quarter of a million school children experiencing literary poverty', www.booktrust.org.uk/news-and-features/news/news-2020/more-than-a-quarter-of-a-million-school-children-experiencing-literary-poverty
Caviglioli, O. (2003), *Think it – Map it!* London: Continuum.
Department for Education (2019), 'School workforce in England: November 2018', www.gov.uk/government/statistics/school-workforce-in-england-november-2018
Department for Education (2020), 'Permanent and fixed-period exclusions in England: 2018 to 2019', www.gov.uk/government/statistics/permanent-and-fixed-period-exclusions-in-england-2018-to-2019
Downes, P. (2002), 'Introduction', in L. Neall, *Bringing the Best Out in Boys*. Stroud: Hawthorne Press.
Education Endowment Foundation (2016), 'Texting Parents', https://educationendowmentfoundation.org.uk/projects-and-evaluation/projects/texting-parents/
Education Endowment Foundation (2018), *Sutton Trust-EEF Teaching and Learning Toolkit*, https://educationendowmentfoundation.org.uk/evidence-summaries/teaching-learning-toolkit/
Fogg, A. (2018), 'What's the problem with white working class boys?', *Politics.co.uk*, www.politics.co.uk/comment-analysis/2018/01/09/what-s-the-problem-with-white-working-class-boys
Ginott, H. (1972), *Teacher and Child: A book for parents and teachers*. New York, NY: The Macmillan Company.
Hargreaves, D. H. (1982), *The Challenge for the Comprehensive School*. Abingdon: Routledge.
House of Commons Library (2020), 'UK Prison Population Statistics', https://commonslibrary.parliament.uk/research-briefings/sn04334/
Hughes, M. (2002), *Tweak to Transform*. London: Continuum.
Jackson, C. (2006), *'Lads' and 'ladettes' in School: Gender and a fear of failure*. Maidenhead: Open University Press.
Kovačević, M., Kraljević, J. and Cepanec, M. (2006), 'Sex differences in lexical and grammatical development in Croatian', Proceedings from the First European Network Meeting on the Communicative Development Inventories. Gävle, Gävle University Press.
O'Connor, R. M. and Waddell, S. (2015), 'What works to prevent gang involvement, youth violence and crime'. London: Early Intervention Foundation.
Ofsted (2019), 'Safeguarding children and young people in education from knife crime', www.gov.uk/government/publications/knife-crime-safeguarding-children-and-young-people-in-education
Robinson, P. and Smithers, A. (1999), 'Should the sexes be separated for secondary education – comparisons of single-sex and co-educational schools?', *Research Papers in Education*, 14, (1), 23-49.

References

Shoemaker, J. (2003), 'What is the best thing a teacher-librarian can do to encourage boys to read?', *Teacher Librarian*, 30, 3.

Smith, M. W. and Wilhelm, J. D. (2002), *Going with the Flow: How to engage boys (and girls) in their literacy learning*. Portsmouth, NH: Heinemann.

Topping, K. (2017), 'What kids are reading: The book-reading habits of pupils in British schools'. London: Renaissance, https://doc.renlearn.com/KMNet/R60818.pdf

West, P. (2002), *What is the Matter with Boys?* Marrickville, NSW: Choice Books.

Wilson, G. (2013), *Breaking Through Barriers to Boys' Achievement: Developing a caring masculinity*. London: Bloomsbury Education.

Younger, M., Warrington, M., Gray, J., Rudduck, J., McLellan, R., Bearne, E., Kershner, R. and Bricheno, P. (2005), 'Raising boys' achievement'. London: Department for Education and Skills, https://dera.ioe.ac.uk/5400/1/RR636.pdf

Index

ability labelling 80
academic setting 77
   impact of 77–9
   misallocation 79–80
   moving up 80
   grouping pupils within a class 81
after-school detentions 178
'Anti-Bullying Massif' 73
anti-social behavior 177

barriers, to education 135
   injustices 136–7
   relationships 136
   reputation, judging on 137
Biddulph, Stephen 132
Big Ears Day 154–5
black ink, writing with 114
Book Trust 117, 29
boy–girl seating 84
boys' audit 159–60
breaks, during lesson 126
bullying 73, 150

challenge versus competition 131–3
change 163–4
   it's never too late 164–5
   year 11s advice to year 7s 165–6
Change Talks 150
Changemakers 155–61
classroom, boys' engagement in 179
communication
   at home 32–4
   importance of 88
competitiveness 131–3
computer games, addiction to 30–2
copying out 111–12, 178
creative writing 179

Dahl, Roald 121
detentions 65–6, 178
   alternatives to 67–8
Downes, Peter 88
drug culture 150

eating at the table 29–30
Educating Yorkshire 49
Education Endowment Foundation (EEF) 77, 79, 80, 96
empowerment 154–61
expert advice 134

fairness 137
feedback 99
five minutes' practice, for handwriting 114

gender, on the agenda 11–12
   Gender and Achievement Working Party (GAWP) 12, 13–14
   meeting with girls 12–13
   Pyramid GAWP 16
   Top Lads 14–15
genuine human interest, of teachers 134, 172
good news noticeboards 170–1
good teacher 47
   being real 49
   importance of gender 49–50
   PE teachers 50–1
   qualifications for 51–3
   respect and consistency 47–9
grouping of pupils 81
group work and discussions 126–7, 178
grunt culture 32
guns 151–2

handwriting 112–15
Hargreaves 80
help 129
   challenge versus competition 131–3
   experts' advice 134

genuine human interest 134
giving boys the big picture 130
praise 133-4
exam revision 130-1
Higgins, Steven 81
high expectations 147
Homerton Report 37, 92-3
home-school communication 56
homework 95, 178
   and home-school relationships 96-8
   points for setting 99
   relevancy of 96
   solutions for issues of 98-9
   value of 99

inclusion 64
independence, of children 29
injustice, as educational barrier 136
inner London school (case study)
   context 175
   methodology 176
   report 176-80
   results 180
interactive lessons 178

Jackson, Carolyn 132
judging on reputation, educational barrier 137

knives 151-2

labelling 19-20
   ability labelling 80
   impact of 21-3
   negative labels 19-20
   positive labels 20
labels stick 21-3
laddish behaviour 40
lessons 125
   breaks 126
   checklist 128
   group work and discussions 126-7
   interactive lessons 178
   memorable lesson 126
   practical lessons 126
   teacher's opinion on 127-8
   teacher's role 127
libraries 29, 117-18
listening skills 61-2

literature-based activities, for reading 121-2
Longfield, Anne 64
love 89

male role models, importance of 29
male teachers, proportion of 40
memorable lesson 126
mentoring 167
   National Education Breakthrough Programme 167-8, 172, 173
   process of 169-73
misallocation, in setting 79-80
mixed-attainment groups 81
motivation, guide for 173

National Education Breakthrough Programme 59, 164, 167-8, 172, 173
National Literacy Trust 123
negative comments 90
negative images and messages 17-18
negative labels 19-20

Parent Engagement Project 97
parents 25
   communication at home 32-4
   leaflet to help boys 26
   rewards and behaviour update for 35
   school messages to 34
   sessions of 25-8
   starting early 29-30
   technology issues 30-2
   texting homework details to 97-8
peer police cadets 14, 39 71-2
   giving responsibility to 72
   hassle issues avoidance 74-5
   holding up work in class 74
   in secondary schools 73
   Transformers 72
peer pressure 71
   see also peer police cadets
pen licence 112-13
Penryn College 155-61
phone calls home 56
Pobble 365 132
poems 105-6, 118, 125
positive comments 90
positive feedback, passing on 58-9
positive labels 20
practical lessons 126

praise 133–4
praise postcards 56–7
punishments 63
   alternatives for 67–9
   detentions 65–6
   inclusion 64
   writing as 66–7, 110
pupil self-assessment guide 173
pupils grouping 81, 91–3
pupil voice 153
   Big Ears Day 154–5
   Changemakers 155–61
   empowerment 154–61
   environment and atmosphere 153–4
   questions to guide conversations 154
   student subject learning review 162
   teachers' listening skill 161
Pyramid GAWP 16

quiet approval 57–8

Random Name Generator 103
reading 117–18, 177
   beyond reading for pleasure 124
   literature-based activities 121–2
   positive experiences of 122
   role models 122–4
reading fiction 119
   approaches 120–1
   rationale for 119
reflection 101–3
relationships, as educational barrier 136
reputation, judging on 137
restorative justice 68–9
revision 130–1
rewards 55
   consistency in giving rewards 59–60
   and knowing your class 61
   listening to the boys in your school 61–2
   need for improvement of 176
   phone calls home 56
   positive feedback, passing on 58–9
   praise 133–4
   praise postcards 56–7
   quiet approval 57–8

short-term rewards 58
Robinson, Pamela 93

sanctions, at school and home 68
sarcasm 179
Scandinavia 34, 37
school, barriers in 41–4
seating plans 83
   boy–girl seating 84
   seating arrangements 84–6
   sitting with friends 83–4
self-analysis 146
sexist society 2
short-term rewards 58
short-term targets 58, 161, 179
single-sex grouping 91–3
Smithers, Alan 93
social media, and mental health 150–1
street culture 149, 177
   drug culture 150
   knives and guns 151–2
   social media and mental health 150–1
student subject learning review 162

Tan, Shaun 121
teaching and learning styles 40
teaching pace 176
Titchmarsh, Alan 123
Top Lads 14–15
Topping, Keith 124
trust 145–6
TV addiction 30–1
Tyrer, Sam 150

underachievement 1–2
   barriers in school 41–4
   measures attempted before 38–40
   reasons for 40–1, 141–4

Wilson, Gary 7–9
writing 105–6, 179
   boys' perceptions 106–10
   copying out 111–12
   handwriting 112–15
   as punishment 66–7, 110